Christian Faith
and
Religious Freedom

V. Norskov Olsen

TEACH Services, Inc.
P U B L I S H I N G
www.TEACHServices.com • (800) 367-1844

Copyright © 2016 V. Norskov Olsen

Copyright © 2016 Teach Services, Inc.

ISBN-13: 978-1-57258-118-0 (Paperback)

ISBN-13: 978-1-4796-0713-6 (ePub)

ISBN-13: 978-1-4796-0714-3 (Mobi)

Library of Congress Control Number: 96-60631

Unless otherwise indicated, all Scripture quotations are from the *New American Standard Bible*. Bible texts credited to KJV are from the *King James Version*, to NRSV are from the *New Revised Standard Version*.

TEACH Services, Inc.
P U B L I S H I N G
www.TEACHServices.com • (800) 367-1844

Also by V. Norskov Olsen:

The New Testament Logia on Divorce.
A Study of Their Interpretation from Erasmus to Milton

John Foxe and the Elizabethan Church

Papal Supremacy and American Democracy

Man, The Image of God:
The Divine Design—The Human Condition

Myth and Truth about Church, Priesthood, and Ordination

The New Relatedness for Man and Woman in Christ
A Mirror of the Divine

Acknowledgments

The writer owes a heartfelt thanks to Attorney Alan J. Reinach for his unfailing encouragement and help. As a director of Religious Liberty he coordinated the plans for printing, publishing and distribution of this book.

I am most appreciative of George Knight's willingness to write the Foreword. Being a professor of church history it is a valuable introductory essay which sets the stage for the chapters that follow.

The Epilogue is written by B.B. Beach. Having been an influential champion for religious freedom for decades, it serves as a capstone of the book.

I feel fortunate that Helen F. Little, a veteran editor and English teacher, was willing to do the copy-editorial work.

To Antoinette Yakush-Gaskell, my secretary for many years, I am greatly indebted. Her efficiency made it possible for the manuscript, after many drafts, to be ready for publication.

The relationship with the publisher, TEACH Services, Inc. has been most profitable and pleasant; for this we thank Wayne Reid, the Representative.

Last but not least, by my wife's unfailing support, expressed in so many ways, this book has been made possible.

Table of Contents

Foreword, by George Knight

Religious freedom and the relationship between religion and the state have been issues of the first magnitude since the beginning of earthly history. Governments and religions are the two social institutions that make absolute demands on the loyalties of their citizens and adherents. Both demand undivided allegiance. Yet their demands are at times diametrically opposed. In such cases the religionist is faced with denying the demands of either the church or the state if he or she is to give supreme allegiance to the other.

While that tension has always existed to some extent, it was minimized in traditional societies in which the state had only one religion—often represented by the national god. Yet even in such civilizations the struggle between church and state was not altogether absent. After all, who was to have the final say—the priesthood or the ruler? That tension existed throughout much of Israel's history as an independent nation.

Some nations escaped the worst of the tension between religious and political authority through the acceptance of their ruler as divine. But the problem was never totally absent.

And for some it was acute and perennial. Such was the case of Israel during those periods in which it was dominated by foreign powers. Israel claimed, unlike many of the regional religions of its surrounding culture, that it worshiped Yahweh—creator of heaven and earth. And Israelites were not allowed to worship any other gods or to bow down or to show allegiance to them. As the first two commandments of the Decalogue put it, "You shall have no other gods before Me. You shall not make for yourself an idol, or any likeness of what is in heaven above or on the earth beneath or in the water under the earth. You shall not worship them or serve them; for I, the Lord your God, am a jealous God" (Ex. 20:3– 5).

Those commands and the Israelite belief system put the nation's citizens on a collision course with any political power that might conquer them. Unlike many other religionists of their day, they were not able to switch allegiance to the new national god of the conquerors, nor were they able to bow down to the religio-political symbols of the new rulers. Thus the dilemma of Daniel's three friends on the plain of Dura. Because they were faithful to Yahweh they could not bow down, even though they desired to be faithful citizens. They were caught between the demands of God and those of the state. The result was a punitive death sentence for noncooperation (see Daniel 3).

In a similar manner, the observance of worship rites to a god other than the national deity in the nations of antiquity could be seen as unpatriotic at best and as traitorous at worst. Such activities could also bring stiff punitive action as we find in the case of Daniel in his dealings with the underlings of King Darius in Daniel 6.

Thus, because of the uncompromising absolutist and universal claims of the Hebrew religion, its adherents found church and state issues to be even more problematic than did other ancient religious groups. Christianity, as an extension of Hebrew religion, inherited the profound church/state tensions of the Israelites. They too were a covenant people who could expect God's blessings if they were faithful to their Lord (see Deut. 28– 30; Gal. 3:28, 29). They too could not bow down to the images of other gods or attribute to any earthly ruler the prerogatives of God.

Thus church/state issues have been central to Christianity from its inception. And the correct course of action has not always been easy to decipher and/or carry out.

The New Testament did not leave Christians without guidance on the topic. One of Jesus' most revolutionary and far reaching statements relates to this very topic. He told the Jewish leaders: "Render to Caesar the things that are Caesar's; and to God the things that are God's" (Matt. 22:21).

The most remarkable thing about that statement is not that it implies the separation of church and state (which it does) or that it suggests that God has a claim on His followers beyond the realm of the state (which it also does). To the contrary, the statement is radical because it reserves a realm of allegiance for the state beyond the realm of religion. Even Caesar the conqueror and "enemy" of God's people had his due coming from the worshipers of Yahweh. Paul picks up that line of thought in Romans 13:1–7 when he calls for Christian allegiance to even pagan earthly governors as "servants of God."

But what about those cases where Caesar (or any other earthly ruler) oversteps his legitimate bounds? What is a Christian to do? After all, Christ does not tell us who has priority—God or Caesar. That issue posed no problem for those knowledgeable in Hebrew history and the covenant obligations undergirding that history. The answer was plain—God always took precedence over the government in case of conflict. Thus the apostles could tell their rulers that "we must obey God rather than men" (Acts 5:29).

But sometimes Caesar would not back off. Sometimes the government clamored for its rights to first allegiance. In such cases, in both testaments one's allegiance to God could lead to the death penalty. The same was true in the early church, the medieval era, the Reformation, and post-Reformation periods, and such will be the case, according to Revelation 13, in the final period of earth's history just before the Second Advent of Jesus.

It is no accident that the Bible presents earthly governments as both beautiful idols and as ravaging beasts in its apocalyptic books. The first set of symbols, of course, is from the perspective of rulers, while the latter is from that of persecuted religionists. Government is "good" when it sticks to its proper sphere but "evil" when it oversteps its bounds. But who is to say when it has overstepped its bounds? Who has that kind of authority? Those questions are where the rub comes in, because in the Hebrew tradition that critical function is the prerogative and duty of religion in its prophetic role. And, it should be obvious, such interpretations by religious authorities cannot and must not be taken lightly by earthly governments if they are to maintain respect and control of their constituents. After all, what government can afford to appear less than supreme in its own realm? On the other hand, religionists must take their religious beliefs with the utmost seriousness.

Thus religious liberty and the relationship between church and state have been issues of great importance down through history. It is the theoretical grounding for those issues that Dr. V. Norskov Olsen examines in his first three chapters.

Chapter One examines the theological foundations in terms of the creatorship of God, the dignity and freedom of humanity, and the relational aspect of human nature. The second chapter extends the theological foundation of religious liberty by grounding religious freedom in Christ's life and work and the redemptive and freedom-producing possibilities of His work. Central to understanding the problem between church and state is the cross of Jesus as the basis of all true freedom. Of particular value in Chapter Two is the idea that Christian freedom is both "freedom from" and "freedom for." Too often Christians have merely thought of religious freedom as freedom from oppression rather than freedom for redemptive service

Chapter Three moves the theological foundation of religious freedom beyond Christology to eschatology as the redemptive result of Christ's work. The chapter particularly examines the concept of the two kingdoms set forth in the New Testament and the implications of the Christian's dual citizenship in both the kingdom of heaven and an earthly state.

The theological grounding provided by the first three chapters is an important antidote to the tendency of many to base their arguments on religious freedom and church/state issues on political or constitutional grounds. Dr. Olsen makes an important contribution to our thinking by making us face the theological bedrock of any Christian approach to these topics.

Chapter Four moves into the realm of the history of issues in religious freedom by giving a European survey of church-state relations, including the Protestant Reformation. Chapter Five demonstrates how the various Reformation approaches to the relationship between church and state were replicated in the American colonies. The chapter also examines major documents of the early republic related to the separation of church and state.

The volume's final chapter examines several major pronouncements on religious liberty by international organizations in the twentieth century. Especially helpful is its insightful and balanced analysis of the religious liberty pronouncements of Vatican II. Dr. Olsen has gone beyond the formal declaration into the ramifications of its total context.

We are in debt to V. Norskov Olsen for his helpful analysis and his innovative approach to the topic. His volume will help us put religious liberty on a more solid basis.

George R. Knight, Berrien Springs, Michigan

I
Religious Freedom: The Theological Foundation

In Our Quest For The Meaning And Purpose Of any specific aspect of life we must begin with theology: The word about God and from God. Most appropriately Holy Scripture begins by stating: "In the beginning God." These opening words of the Bible are most profound, telling us that God is the originating source and prime mover of life. They also point to original and true life conditions or constitutive precepts established by the Creator in the beginning; we refer to these as the order of creation.

THE CREATOR GOD AND FREEDOM
It is the unanimous testimony of the Bible that the Almighty God is the Creator and Supreme Lord of all: "The Lord has established His throne in the heaven; And His sovereignty rules over

all." "Worthy art Thou, our Lord and our God, to receive glory and honor and power; for Thou didst create all things, and because of Thy will they existed, and were created" (Ps. 103:19; Rev. 4:11). When we study the history of religious liberty in America we notice that prior to the formulation of the United States Constitution local states had made provision for religious liberty in their respective constitutions; it is significant that they referred to religious liberty and freedom of conscience as a human right and duty owed to the "Creator"[1] and "Almighty God."[2]

Thomas Paine recognized the same as these constitutions in his renowned book, The Rights of Man (1791), in which he defended the constitutional attempts of France and America to guarantee human rights. Wrote Paine: "The error of those who reason by precedents drawn from antiquity, respecting the rights of man, is that they do not go far enough into antiquity. They do not go the whole way. They stop in some of the intermediate stages of an hundred or a thousand years,...but if we proceed on, we shall at last come out right: we shall come to the time when man came from the hand of his maker. What was he then? Man. Man was his high and only title, and a higher cannot be given him."[3]

MAN: THE IMAGE OF GOD

In the creation of man as the image of God we find the theological foundation and thereby the basic and distinct rationale for the recognition and preservation of the rights of religious liberty and freedom of conscience. We will examine a few aspects of the first anthropological statement: "God said, 'Let us make humankind in our image.' So God created humankind in his image, in the image of God he created them" (Gen. 1:26, 27 NRSV).[4]

Since man is to find his existence as the image of God we deal not merely with theology (the word about God) or anthropology (the word about man), but with theoanthropology—that is, the word about God and man between whom there is a close relationship.

THE DIGNITY OF MAN

The preamble to the Universal Declaration of Human Rights by the General Assembly of the United Nations (1948) recognizes that "the inherent dignity" and "the equal and inalienable rights of all members of the human family is the foundation of freedom, justice, and peace in the world."[5]

Francis A. Schaeffer, in A Christian Manifesto, put it accurately when he stated: "We must understand that the question of the dignity of human life is not something on the periphery of Judeo-Christian thinking, but almost in the center of it (though not the center because the center is the existence of God Himself). But the dignity of human life is unbreakably linked to the existence of the personal-infinite God. It is because there is a person-infinite God who has made men and women in His own image that they have a unique dignity of life as human beings."[6]

When we speak about the uniqueness and dignity of man, we are not concerned with one topic among others, but with the primeval and fundamental realities of man. In the incarnation of Jesus Christ—as it later will be observed—is manifested the inestimable value God places upon humankind.

MAN: A MORAL BEING

The Christian world-view begins with God as Creator and Lawgiver. Since God is the Creator and everything is rooted in Him and His activities, it follows that life is based on conformity to, or oneness with, the principles or laws that are imperative to life itself. God's "judgments" are not capricious; they are natural consequences of transgression.

God not only created and blessed humankind, but in His first personal dealing with Adam and Eve "God said" and "the Lord God commanded" (Gen. 1:28; 2:16). At the time of the first temptation it was acknowledged both by the serpent and by Eve that "God has said" (Gen. 3:1, 3). Man was created as a free and self-conscious moral being. Ellen G. White explains: "Our first parents, though created innocent and holy, were not placed beyond the possibility of wrongdoing. God made them free moral agents, capable of appreciating the wisdom and benevolence of his character and the justice of his requirements, and with full liberty to yield or to withhold obedience." Accordingly, "to deprive man of the freedom of choice would be to rob him of his prerogative as an intelligent being, and make him a mere automaton. It is not God's purpose to coerce the will. Man was created a free moral agent."[7]

Man's moral instinct or conscience cannot be accounted for either from the point of view of mechanics or the animal world. However, as pointed out by Joseph Baldwin, "Moral laws regulate the moral universe just as physical laws regulate the physical universe.... Conscience is to the moral universe what gravity is to the world of matter.... Conscience is the law-obeying energy of the soul."[8] Moral evidences show that man's primary obligation is to God as the moral Lawgiver and Ruler; accordingly, Christ said to the tempter in the wilderness, "Begone, Satan! For it is written You shall worship the Lord your God, and serve Him only" (Matt. 4:10). God is the final judge of the individual: "For we must all appear before the judgment seat of Christ" (2 Cor. 5:10).

As God-the-Creator and God-the-Lawgiver are one, so the purpose of life and law go hand in hand. Arthur Holmes writes: "In regard to ethics, therefore, the God-creation relation underscores the value of what God intended for His creation; it alerts us to moral indicators, like natural laws, in the way things are made; it presents us with a mandate—an obligation in fact— to respect human rights. And this has social and political consequences."[9]

Religious freedom is the first human right, for it has to do with man's moral obligations to the Creator and the order (principles, laws) of His creation. Emil Brunner makes a helpful point when he notes: "The emergence of the moral element in human life means that man has realized himself as a person; it means that the whole of life is now regarded from the point of view of decision, self-determination, freedom, responsibility."[10]

THE FREEDOM OF MAN

As a moral being man's constitutive relationship with God is one of freedom. However, man has no independent existence; consequently, freedom cannot stand alone. It has two elements: freedom "from something" and freedom "for something." Thomas Merton in his book No Man is An Island writes: "An act without purpose lacks something of the perfection of freedom, because freedom is more than a matter of aimless choice. It is not enough to affirm my liberty by choosing 'something'. I must use and develop my freedom by choosing something good."[11]

Freedom is often defined as "independence," and false liberalism adheres to this philosophy of freedom. Karl Marx expressed it as a maxim: "Man is free only if he owes his existence to himself." Brunner makes this observation: "In the classless society man owes his existence to himself, and in atheism he becomes aware of the fact that he owes it to himself. Therefore Communism and atheism are linked together in the very foundations of the Marxist system."[12]

The dictionary definition of freedom, as independence, falls very short of the biblical concept of freedom; Brunner affirms that "this conception of freedom does not grasp the centre of personality." He explains: "The centre of personality is our relation to God.... For in relation to God man is the more free as he is the more dependent. Deo servire libertas. The human self is not an entity in itself. Human personality is what it is through its relation to God.... The more man is sufficient unto himself, the less he is free; and the less he suffices for himself and seeks his life and meaning in God, the freer he is."[13]

MAN: A RELIGIOUS BEING

Man was not created for a mere temporal life but to live eternally. God has "set eternity in their [men's] hearts" (Eccl. 3:11). In his talk on Mars Hill, the apostle Paul complimented the Athenians for being "very religious in all respects." Then, having made reference to the inscription on one of their many polytheistic altars, "To An Unknown God," Paul asserted, "What therefore you worship in ignorance, this I proclaim to you." He explains that God "Himself gives to all life and breath and all things," and that men "should seek God, if perhaps they might grope for him and find Him, though He is not far from each one of us; for in Him we live and move and exist" (Acts 17:22– 28).

Anthropology testifies to the universality of the concept of a god even though not a clearly understood concept. Professor M. Valentine asserted in his writings: "We are safe in saying that there has been found no well authenticated case of a nation or race utterly without some conception of deity or conviction of the existence of a Supreme Being."[14] Arnold Toynbee wrote in An Historian's Approach to Religion, "Religion is an essential element in Human Life which cannot ever be ignored or repressed for very long at a time."[15] In our own time the collapse of Communism verifies the truth of this statement.

The uniqueness of the eternal longing in man's heart tells us that man was intended to be more than a finite being. Religion as a personal relationship with God is at the heart of true humanness and a natural condition of life. Church Father Augustine in the opening paragraph of his autobiography, Confessions, expresses this thought in the classic aphorism: "God, thou hast made us for Thyself and restless is our heart until it comes to rest in Thee."

MAN: A RELATIONAL BEING

The biblical concept of God is Trinitarian. The Trinity are personalities in harmony and interrelatedness. Both on the divine and human level personhood exists in relationships.

Man is so created that he can in freedom enter into a mutual relationship with God. It is only in communion God that his true humanness can be realized. From the divine-human relationship grows a three-dimensional relationship which form an inseparable unity: God to man, man to man, and man to God.

Christ declares that there is a twofold relational commandment: "You shall love the Lord your God with all your heart and with all your soul, and with all your mind.... you shall love your neighbor as yourself" (Matt. 22:37, 39). Loving one's neighbor means that we respect his individuality and freedom as God does. Christ makes a further explanation: "Therefore, however you want people to treat you, so treat them, for this is the Law and the Prophets" (Matt. 7:12). The great commandment likewise points out the social responsibility for the one in need. Speaking to those who will inherit the kingdom of God, Christ tells us that they, as relational beings, will meet the social needs of the neighbor who is thirsty, hungry, naked, sick, a prisoner, a stranger, etc. (see Matt. 25:21– 46).

Our fellowmen are all the children of God and our relationship to our "neighbor" cannot be separated from our relationship to God. Christ concludes His comments on this theme by stating: "Truly I say to you, to the extent that you did it to one of these brothers of Mine, even the least of them, you did it to Me.... Truly I say to you, to the extent that you did not do it to one of the least of these, you did not do it to Me" (Matt. 25:40,45). The one who cannot "love his brother whom he has seen, cannot love God whom he has not seen. And this commandment we have from Him, that the one who loves God should love his brother also" (1 John 4:20– 21; see also 3:17; 4:12).

By meeting the need of the oppressed and creating freedom for opportunity to help—everywhere in the world—the Christians are serving the Creator, Who is desirous to see relief extended to men and women in want and bondage of many kinds. Divine relatedness is constituted in "mutual otherness," and should be mirrored in the human relatedness where religious liberty pragmatically creates "freedom from" and "freedom for" the neighbor as stipulated by Christ.

In an article "Toward the Heart of the Matter," Eberhard Jüngel succinctly writes: "The Trinitarian being of God, which I understand as a community of mutual otherness, could be an incentive to develop models of earthly being-together: vestigia trinitatis [imprints of the Trinity], as it were, in which creatures would be enabled to exist in communities of mutual otherness (this could also be relevant for political ethics). To be sure, the kingdom of God wouldn't thereby be brought about. But in spite of that, the earth would be protected from becoming hell."[16]

The questions could be raised: Does society exist for the individual or does the individual exist for the society? The truth is that the good of the individual and that of society can be realized only in proper relationships. Accordingly, the Lord's Prayer is a common prayer: "Our Father.... Give us.... Forgive us.... Lead us not.... Deliver us."

The nature of man is such that he cannot, as a relational being, realize his gift of life except in society, but the society cannot be true to its purpose unless the dignity, moral consciousness, religious freedom, and individuality of man are preserved in the light of the understanding of humankind as "the image of God."

II

Religious Freedom:
The Christological Foundation

"If therefore the Son shall make you free, you shall be free indeed" (John 8:36). These words by Christ express comprehensively the significance of the Christological foundation of religious freedom, and are echoed by the apostle Paul: "It was for freedom that Christ set us free" (Gal. 5:1).

THE SON OF MAN: THE IMAGE OF GOD
Through the incarnation Jesus Christ became the Son of Man—the man par excellence—and the representative of humankind. He is referred to as the second or new Adam (Rom. 5:14; 1 Cor. 15:22, 45, 47). In the Son of Man the image of God was restored in humankind and thereby the genuine principles of religious freedom established anew. The apostle Paul speaks about "the light of the gospel of the glory of Christ, who is

the image of God" (2 Cor. 4:4) and tells us that God has "delivered us from the domain of darkness, and transferred us to the kingdom of His beloved Son, in whom we have redemption, the forgiveness of sins. And He is the image of the invisible God" (Col. 1:13– 15). Similarly, it is expressed that Christ "is the radiance" of God's "glory and the exact representation of His nature" (Heb. 1:3).

All what God has to say about Himself is personified in Jesus Christ, who stated about Himself, "He who has seen Me has seen the Father" (John 14:9). The inescapable conclusion is that true freedom (from something and for something) in man's inner and outer world has found its full and true realization in Jesus Christ. There is an obvious correlation between the renewal of the image of God and genuine freedom attained in Jesus Christ as the center of our lives; both can be claimed and realized by humankind only by faith in Him. We will take note of this.

RELIGIOUS FREEDOM AND CHRISTIAN FAITH

"Religious liberty is the foundation and guardian of all human rights," wrote A. F. Carrillo De Albornoz, Secretariat for Religious Liberty, World Council of Churches (WCC). This statement is similarly expressed in official ecumenical declarations: "Religious freedom is the foundation of all freedom." "Religious freedom is the condition and guardian of all true freedom." The reason given by the Central Committee of WCC for these statements is that "the fundamental rights of the human person cannot endure except when they are acknowledged as derived from man's relation to God in Christ."[1]

Other ecumenical statements assert that religious freedom is "an implication of the faith of the church," "an implication of the Christian faith," and "has its deepest foundations in the gospel of Jesus Christ." Accordingly, the subject of religious freedom must be framed within "the full meaning and nature of the gospel."[2]

During the formative and formulative period of WCC, two influential essays dealing with the theological and biblical basis

for religious liberty, were written, one by the theologian Niels H.
Soe and one by the New Testament scholar Amos N. Wilder. Both
emphasized Christology as the constituent part of religious liberty. Professor Soe pointed out that the basis is found "in the very
centre of the Christian message, in the very way it pleased God to
bring to us his saving act." He explains: "The basis of religious liberty is the very fact that Christ did not come in heavenly splendour
and worldly majesty to subjugate any possible resistance and force
all and everybody to subjection. Christ made himself of no reputa-
tion and took upon him the form of a servant and humbled himself
even unto the death of the cross. When the Pharisees approached
him and said: We would see a sign from thee, he refrained from
fulfilling a request like that. Instead of a sign which might have
been an indubitable proof of his lordship he pointed to his preaching and told them of this preaching that it was greater than that
of the prophet Jonas, and of his wisdom which surpassed that of
Solomon. Never did he do anything to force people into obedience and submission. Finally he was crucified through weakness,
as Paul has it. And even when he rose from the dead he did not
show himself alive to those who had brought him to the cross that
so they might finally bow their knees and surrender to him. He
sent out his disciples without any kind of worldly power or force."[3]

Soe asks the question: "Why did saving, divine revelation
come in this meek and humble way and so lay itself open to
human refusal, resistance and even scorn?" The answer is love,
which "wants fellowship, communion with the beloved one....
The free choice, the possibility of choosing unbelief, choosing to
be offended in Jesus because of his unsightly state, Jesus himself
could not take that away because of his love. Had he done so,
he would have frustrated his own purpose.... Love is inseparable
from respect of the other's personality. Divine love, strange as it
may seem, is not different in that sense. God wants communion
with man. And therefore wills that man remain man, a personal,
responsible being."[4]

In the light of this it is understandable that Soe, as a member of the WCC Commission on Religious Liberty, advised that

"it is not single passages in the Bible, it is Christ's whole way of approaching mankind that gives us our lead."[5]

Professor Wilder affirmed the same: "The dignity or rights or value of men as the children of God and as loved by him should be understood in the context of the Cross if they are to have their full significance and if we are to avoid a secularization leading either to banality or destructive illusions."[6]

It has been pointed out that in the past "American thinkers preferred to deal with juridical and political arguments in favor of religious freedom, while European authors…study almost exclusively its biblical and theological basis." It is suggested that the reason for this is that from the American point of view "religious freedom has no special problem of its own, and that this question should be satisfactorily resolved on the juridical, canonical, and political level." Having described the two views Carrillo De Albornoz expresses a certain warning. He writes: "We cannot help feeling that, if the American tendency prevails, the deep theological meaning of religious liberty would be lost and also that religious rights of man could suffer (above all in times of so-called emergencies) the same destiny as many other human rights or constitutional guarantees."[7] Obviously, a Christological foundation is most relevant for religious freedom.

THE CROSS AND RELIGIOUS FREEDOM

In the very beginning God enacted the covenant of life (which embodied the very principles of life); at the same time He also established the covenant of redemption. This meant that in the case of transgression (with its result of death), God would, in Jesus Christ, take upon Himself the consequences of breaching the covenant of life. In spite of the disintegrating effects of the original Fall of humankind, there is hope of a new order.

The covenant of life—obey and live, disobey and die—could not be eliminated for humankind is a free, moral being, and that could not be altered. In the case of transgression death would come as a natural consequence, but the promise of forgiveness by grace came in alongside law. In Jesus Christ humankind is brought into a renewed relationship with God through the covenant of redemption. Christ is said to be "the Lamb slain from the foundation of the world" (Rev. 13:8 KJV).

On the cross of Calvary we see righteousness and grace, justice and mercy blended. John Stott concisely states that the cross of Christ was "divine self-satisfaction through divine self-substitution." Stott explains that the Creator, "was unwilling to act in love at the expense of his holiness or in holiness at the expense of his love. So we may say that he satisfied his love by himself dying the death and so bearing the judgment which sinners deserved. He both exacted and accepted the penalty of human sin."[8]

The same is expressed by G. E. Berkouwer in these words: "If anything is clear in the biblical revelation it is certainly that the cross is the revelation of God's love but also, at the same time, of his holiness and justice." The cross "shows us that sin was atoned for precisely because it was also condemned. Thus the gospel is a fountain of knowledge for our sins as well as our forgiveness."[9]

The gospel tells us that in the cross of Christ is found the freedom from the ominous results of the Fall; likewise, Calvary is the fountainhead for power to apply the true principles of life so that the original intent of "freedom for" may be realized. In the light of this it is understandable, as previously observed, that religious liberty is considered "an implication of the Christian faith," has its "foundation in the gospel" and "should be understood in the context of the Cross."

The twofold freedom of the cross of Christ (freedom from, freedom for) is expressed by Christ and the apostle Paul in two meaningful expressions. Christ said, "Abide in Me, and I in you" (John 15:4). In his epistles Paul speaks about "being in Christ" more than 150 times. For example, he writes, "There is therefore now no condemnation for those who are in Christ Jesus" (Rom. 8:1). The one "in Christ Jesus" is covered by Christ's righteousness and is free from condemnation, guilt, fear, and anxiety. In this way a person obtains an inner freedom, the basis for all freedom. The apostle also speaks about "Christ in you" as in the statement,

"Christ in you, the hope of glory" (Col. 1:17). Of his own experience Paul said, "It is no longer I who live, but Christ lives in me" (Gal. 2:20). "For to me, to live is Christ" (Phil. 1:21). For Paul the "freedom for" (be an image of God) is, like "freedom from," only possible by total dependence upon the grace of Christ manifested for man in forgiveness and renewal.

The principle of freedom in Jesus Christ is named "the Spirit of life in Christ Jesus," and it will "set you free from the law of sin and of death." Accordingly, Paul speaks about "the freedom of the glory of the children of God" (Rom. 8:2, 21). We further read, "Where the Spirit of the Lord is, there is liberty." "It was for freedom that Christ set us free...you were called to freedom" (2 Cor. 3:17, Gal. 5:1, 13).

The Christian religion is not merely theocentric, or God-centered, but is most uniquely Christ-centered. Here lies the fundamental difference between Christianity and other religions. Further, Christianity is Christian only in proportion to its full and correct understanding of Jesus Christ. This understanding is described by the apostle Paul as "wisdom, however, not of this age, nor of the ruler of this age, who are passing away" (1 Cor. 2:6). Christ's redemptive activities mean freedom from the sinister cause of the Fall and degenerating results of not being in harmony with the order of creation. The wholeness of God's redemptive act includes both reconciliation and restoration, or renewal. In this twofold Christian experience faith itself is dynamic and re-creative.

CHRIST AND THE INDIVIDUAL

When we study the life of Christ we cannot help but be impressed with His high regard for the dignity of each individual. He saw in each person a precious child of God; accordingly, He sought to redeem (give freedom to) the outcast, the neglected, the prisoner, the sick, etc. In all His activities Christ was person-motivated and the sovereignty of the individual was at the center of His teaching and activities.[10]

In the Sermon on the Mount Christ gives the assurance that God cares for each individual: "Look at the birds of the air, that they do not sow, neither do they reap, nor gather into barns, and yet your heavenly Father feeds them Are you not worth much more than they? But if God so arrays the grass of the field, which is alive today and tomorrow is thrown into the furnace, will He not much more do so for you, O men of little faith?" (Matt. 6:26, 30). God's concern for the individual is also expressed in these words: "But the very hairs of your head are all numbered" (Matt. 10:30). In this connection we will note the words of A. F. Carrillo De Albornoz: "Religious freedom, although really a human right, is nevertheless on a higher level than other human rights, as it is based directly upon the absolute relation of man to God."[11]

The criterion for entering the kingdom is doing "the will of My Father," said Christ; but in all responses to His will, in different ways and at different times, God works with each person individually. In the Gospel of John we see Christ relating to Nathanial, Nicodemus, the woman of Samaria, and the woman taken in adultery, each in a difference manner. Because He was interested in their personal response, Christ took His disciples apart from the masses and asked them, "But who do you say that I am?" (Matt. 16:15). While Christ sought to sanctify the character of the disciples, He never attempted to rob them of their individuality. Clear evidence of Christ's protection of a person's individual freedom of choice is shown by the fact that Judas was not forced to do right simply by being associated with Christ. Paul's instruction to the early Christian church placed much emphasis on the freedom and responsibility of the individual conscience as he admonished the members to refrain from judging one another's Christian experience (Col. 2:16). Men are converted to God as individuals and sanctified as individuals. Each person, as an individual, has an eternal destiny; this cannot be said about civilizations, cultures, or societies, which are temporal.

Dealing with the individual's ultimate responsibility to God, Wilder put the issue succinctly when he wrote: "The relation of the self to God is of such a kind that it escapes the jurisdiction of human instances and authorities. Human authorities, whether state or church, should not trespass upon this final zone of liberty of the creature in what concerns his destiny and his dealings with eternity."[12]

FREEDOM AND VOLUNTARYISM

Since a person's relationship to the Creator is one of freedom, it follows that his service for God is voluntary. As a consequence the collective group of Christians must be a free church, that is, without coercion from the outside. Franklin H. Littell correctly concludes: "Voluntaryism and religious liberty rest upon the profound understanding that religious service only is pleasing to God which is voluntary and uncoerced. In pre-biblical religions, the gods were used by men to hold society together, to bless political systems and even military conquest. In the Bible, however, God requires obedience and service to His purpose—and He even creates a people whose very existence is based on that function."[13] Littell also points out: "Politically speaking, the principle of voluntaryism is the positive side of opposition to state interference in affairs of the Church. The contribution of the Free Churches has been not only in spreading the principle of voluntaryism abroad in an open society characterized by a wide variety of free institutions, but in developing certain patterns of internal health from which that society derives direct benefit."[14]

Christian voluntaryism is constituted in the love of God and in the love to God. This is very concisely expressed by Ellen G. White: "The law of love being the foundation of the government of God, the happiness of all created beings depended upon their perfect accord with its great principles of righteousness. God desires from all His creatures the service of love,—homage that springs from an intelligent appreciation of His character. He takes no pleasure in a forced allegiance, and to all He grants freedom of will, that they may render Him voluntary service."[15]

As one of our closing comments we will refer to G. C. Berkouwer, who quotes H. Schlier saying, "In the Christian idea of

freedom the breakthrough to real freedom occurs. If we comprehend what freedom is in its Christian meaning, then we have also
grasped the source of every freedom."[16] Accordingly, religious liberty is defined as the "first freedom" and "the first human right."

Juridical, canonical, political, ethical, social, historical, and
biblically prophetic arguments have—and for good reason—been
employed to substantiate religious freedom. However, the Christological foundation of religious freedom is based on an evaluation
which asks whether or not all the components making up religious
freedom are Christ-originated, Christ-founded, Christ-motivated,
Christ-oriented, Christ-spirited, Christ-approved, Christ-centered, and Christ-like. As we began this chapter so will we close
by citing Christ's own words: "If therefore the Son shall make you
free, you shall be free indeed" (John 8:36). The Pauline assertion
holds true: "For no man can lay a foundation other than the one
which is laid, which is Jesus Christ" (1 Cor. 3:11).

III

The Two Kingdoms: Contrasting Spheres of Existence

The Christian principles of religious freedom are practiced within a biblical framework of a great cosmic conflict between good and evil. In this conflict Christians "have become a spectacle to the world, both to angels and to men" (1 Cor. 4:9). The cosmic struggle began when mankind broke the God-given covenant of life. Transgression (sin) broke the relationship with God. Sin is not merely an ethical and juridical fact; it is an ominous event. We refer to this event as the Fall of man; the power of death became a reality. The long and sad history of mankind attests to the tragic results of the Fall. Life and death, good and evil, Christ and Satan became opposing operative forces in man's state of being. The Bible speaks of the two contrasting spheres of existence as kingdoms.

PILATE AND THE KINGDOM OF GOD

When Christ was summoned before the judgment seat of Pilate, the latter asked Christ, "Are You the King of the Jews?" Jesus replied, "My kingdom is not of this world. If My kingdom were of this world, then My servants would be fighting, that I might not be delivered up to the Jews; but as it is, My kingdom is not of this realm." Pilate then said, "So You are a king?" Jesus responded, "You say correctly that I am a king. For this I have been born, and for this I have come into the world, to bear witness to the truth. Everyone who is of the truth hears My voice." Jesus' answer prompted Pilate to ask Christ, "What is truth?" To the Jews Pilate said, "I find no guilt in Him" (John 18:33–38). The latter he repeated twice (John 19:4, 6). When Pilate finally gave in to the request that Christ should be crucified, we are told, "he took water and washed his hands in front of the multitude, saying, 'I am innocent of this man's blood; see to that yourselves.' And all the people answered and said, 'His blood be on us and our children' " (Matt. 27:24–25).

In Pilate's examination of Christ one thing seems clear: Pilate perceived that Christ's kingship and kingdom were in the spiritual or religious realm, and not political in nature. Further, the crucifixion of Christ brings into focus Christ's concept of church-state relationships: "Render to Caesar the things that are Caesar's; and to God the things that are God's" (Matt. 22:21).

TWO CHURCH-STATE CONCEPTS IN JUDAISM

In the Gospels we read over and over again that Christ had encounters with two groups of people: the Sadducees and the Pharisees. Each group or party had its own church-state concept, but both differed from that of Christ's.

The priestly aristocracy was made up of the Sadducees. Accordingly we read that the high priest and associates belonged to "the sect of the Sadducees" (Acts. 5:17). The political affairs of the country were in their hands and they sought in every respect to cooperate with and were subservient to the Romans. Professor

Oscar Cullmann, in his penetrating study The State in the New Testament, tells us that "the Sadducees, assented without reservation to the Roman domination, surrendering all hope of the Kingdom of God. The Sadducees are indeed the collaborationists of that time. They were agreeable to every excess of executive power on the part of the Romans."[1] During the history of Christianity that type of linkage between the priesthood and the secular authorities eventually led to the establishment of a state-church.

The Pharisees, on the other hand, believed in a Jewish theocracy. On account of this, "they had to renounce the State unreservedly."[2] This fact was given its strongest expression by the Zealots and let to the Jewish war with the Romans and the destruction of Jerusalem, AD 70. Oscar Cullman writes: "Jesus agrees with Zealotism insofar as it takes seriously the expectation of the Kingdom of God and thus does not regard the existing Roman State as an ultimate, divine institution. On the other hand he radically divorces himself from the Zealots insofar as they intend to establish the Kingdom of God on their own by human strength, insofar as they do not acknowledge that this age, with the institution of the State, is willed by God. They have a false expectation of the Kingdom of God. Therefore they want to initiate a holy war and to establish within a human framework a Kingdom of God which is an earthly kingdom and which at the same time takes the place of the Roman Empire."[3]

Prior to the crucifixion of Christ the disciples of Christ lacked the understanding of the nature of the Kingdom of Christ, as reflected in Peter's use of the sword in the Garden of Gethsemane and his denial of being a disciple of Christ.

In the crucifixion of Christ the Roman State, the Sadducees, and the Pharisees transgressed, each in their own way, the God-given principles of religious freedom and church-state relationships. In spite of the fact that Pilate knew that the Jews accused Christ for religious reasons and that judgment of religious matters was outside the jurisdiction of Caesar, he nevertheless gave in to the political pressure of the Sadducees and Pharisees, who in spite of their opposing religious views, made a common political move against Christ.

The Sadducees never forgot nor forgave Christ's cleansing of the temple when He said that they had made the temple "a Robbers Den." From that time the chief priests "began seeking how to destroy Him; for they were afraid of Him, for all the multitude was astonished at His teaching" (Mk. 11:17– 18). The Sadducees' relationship to the Roman state made it only natural that the high priests sought its help against Christ and said to Pilate, "We have no king but Caesar" (John 19:15).

When the Pharisees joined the high priests in the appeal to Pilate against Christ, they compromised their theocratic concept: a state governed by God alone.

The political church-state ramifications for Christ's crucifixion tells us that there is a correlation between religious freedom and separation of church and state. We have observed the Christological foundation of the former, but the crucifixion of Christ—so central to Christianity—points to a cruel disregard for the Christological foundation of church-state separation.

THE NATURE OF THE KINGDOM OF GOD

Caesar rules in the strength of God's judgment over sin, that is, by death, and is represented by the sword. The French philosopher Blaire Pascal is said to have declared: "The moldering kingdoms built of iron and blood preach about sin and judgment better than any evangelist." It should not surprise us that in the Old and New Testaments the historical worldpowers are depicted as wild and ugly beasts (see Dan. 7; Rev. 13, 16:13, 19:20, 20:10). Christ exchanged the iron sword of Caesar with the sword of the Spirit. The only weapon the church has is the Word of God, "For the Word of God is living and active and sharper than any two-edged sword, and piercing as far as the division of soul and spirit, of both joints and marrow, and able to judge the thoughts and intentions of the heart" (Heb. 4:12). Accordingly, Paul states that "the weapons of our warfare are not of the flesh, but divinely powerful for the destruction of fortresses. We are destroying speculations and every lofty thing raised up against the knowledge of God, and we are taking every thought captive to the obedience of Christ" (2 Cor. 10:4– 5).

The mother of James and John came to Jesus with a bold request. "She said to Him, Command that in Your kingdom these two sons of mine may sit, one on Your right and one on Your left.' " This request reflects the attitude of the Zealots. In response, Jesus taught the 12 disciples a basic principle of the kingdom of God. Said Jesus: "You know that the rulers of the Gentiles lord it over them, and their great men exercise authority over them. It is not so among you, but whoever wishes to become great among you shall be your servant, and whoever wishes to be first among you shall be your slave; just as the Son of Man did not come to be served, but to serve…" (Matt. 20:21, 25– 28).

The kingdom of God is not a domain, but the rule of God. In this fallen world it is a 180-degree turnaround in the concepts of values as proclaimed in the Sermon on the Mount: Blessed are the poor in spirit, those who mourn, who are gentle, merciful—theirs is the kingdom.

As we study the lives of the disciples of Christ, it becomes obvious that the concept of self-forgetful service as the highest realization of self, was something new for them and contrary to the behavior of man. That was not the kingdom they expected. It is therefore no wonder that Christ spoke about the need to be converted and to "be born again" in order to enter the kingdom of God. The promulgation of the nature of the kingdom of God was illustrated by Christ in the parable of a seed planted in the soil. The seed disintegrates but gives birth to a new life; thus, by losing self in service within the sphere of the kingdom of God, a new life begins, resulting in the fullest realization of the very self of man.

To Pilate Christ said, "I am a king." In the person of Christ the promised kingdom of the Old Testament entered into history. The hoped-for peace of the Old Testament was fulfilled in Christ as Prince of Peace. "There will be no end to the increase of His government or of peace" (Isa. 9:7). At His triumphant entrance into

Jerusalem, the people shouted with great joy, "Blessed is the King who comes in the name of the Lord; Peace in heaven and glory in the highest!" (Luke 19:38). It is of interest to notice that to those whom Christ made whole He said, "Go in peace" (Luke 7:50). No wonder that the apostle Paul called Christ "our peace," and the message about Him the "gospel of Peace" (Eph. 2:14, 6:15). During the Passion Week Christ said to His disciples: "Peace I leave with you; My peace I give to you; not as the world gives, do I give to you. Let not your heart be troubled, nor let it be fearful" (John 14:27).

The Greek words translated "to make peace" signify "to bind together." The negative, or opposite, meaning of the Greek word for peace means "to be out of joint." With this in mind, we can better comprehend the significance of the word peace in Colossians 1:19, 20: "For it was the Father's good pleasure...through Him to reconcile all things to Himself, having made peace through the blood of His cross." At the cross everything out of joint was brought into joint again, for there Christ "made peace." At the foot of the cross all that is out of joint in our inner and social lives can be brought back into proper relationship again—that is, brought into harmony with the kingdom of God.

In his book Freedom Today Hans Küng concludes his discussion on the freedom of the individual by asking a question: "What, then, is the real point for a Christian in the world?" We will quote his answer, appropriate as it is to our discussion. He writes: "To make a radical choice in faith, despite all our sinfulness and to sustain it through ordinary daily life, for God the Lord and his kingdom. To keep, in the world, one's fundamental freedom from the world, in the midst of one's family, one's possessions and the State, in service of God and of one's brothers. To be cheerfully ready at any time to embody this freedom in renunciation, even, when called on for it, in total renunciation. It is only in this freedom from the world, in the world, for God the Lord, given by God's grace, that the Christian can find strength, consolation, power, joy-victory."[4]

THE ESCHATOLOGY OF THE KINGDOM
OF GOD

The kingdom of Christ is His spiritual rule in the hearts of men and it is present in the church, which bears witness to Christ's kingdom. In this way the kingdom of God was inaugurated and its citizens "have tasted the good word of God and the power of the age to come" (Heb. 6:5). Presently the power of the new age of Christ is in tension and struggle with the power of the old age; accordingly, the life under the kingdom of Christ is also directed to the consummation at the second advent of Christ when "every tongue should confess that Jesus Christ is Lord, to the glory of God the Father" (Phil. 2:11). Then "the kingdom of the world has become the kingdom of our Lord, and of His Christ, and He will reign forever and ever" (Rev. 11:15; see also 12:10; Dan. 7:14). Those who lived under the kingship of Christ will on that day hear the voice of the King: "Inherit the kingdom prepared for you from the foundation of the world" (Matt. 25:34).

In the ancient world man had little concept of history. He understood history merely as a circular repetition of events. The uniqueness of the Hebrew prophets' concepts of history was linear, climaxing in the appearance of the Son of man. In the same painting a landscape painter may portray a village, with its houses and people in the foreground, and in the background a valley and hills, sky and sun, even though some are a very great distance away. In their description of the future the Bible writers likewise depict the first and second advents of Christ, the first in the foreground and the latter in the background of salvation history.

The biblical hope does not move in a circle, with one center, around the first or the second advent of Christ; it moves as in an ellipse, which has two foci, around both events, inseparably. The New Testament writers expressed strong faith in a fully realized hope at the second advent as the climactic result of the redemptive accomplishments of Christ's first advent. It is therefore with good reason that emphasis should be placed upon the eschatological aspects of church-state relationships.

Making reference to the words "for our citizenship is in heaven, from which also we eagerly wait for a Savior, the Lord Jesus Christ" (Phil. 3:20); "For here we do not have a lasting city, but we are seeking the city which is to come" (Heb. 13:14) Cullman speaks about the believers as "the community of the coming age" and states: "The fact that the problem of church and state is of such central importance is a corollary of the eschatological attitude of Christianity." In the eschatological aspect is found an inherent dualism. Cullmann explains: "It is really false to understand the Christian expectation of the end as if it were equivalent to indifference to present earthly values. On the contrary: from the Christian expectation of the end proceed very strong impulses toward dealings with the world. Christian eschatology does not mean simply 'denial of the world,' nor, to be sure, 'affirmation of the world.' "5

CHURCH-STATE DUALISM

The dualism of church and state is rooted in the belief that the kingdom of God is eternal but the state is temporal. Cullmann affirms: "The relationship of the Christian to the State is accordingly expressed first of all in temporal categories: the State appears as something 'provisional'. For this reason we do not find anywhere in the New Testament a renunciation of the State as such as a matter of principle; but neither do we find an uncritical acceptance—as if the State itself were something final, definitive."6

The state's lack of understanding of the nature of the Kingdom of God and the Christian hope has often led to persecution. It should also be mentioned that false and militant eschatological movements have neither understood the same and have brought discredit to Christianity and justifiable state-intervention. The following observation amplifies this point: "The Christians' expectation of the End has been even further misconstrued, as if Christians were enemies of the State on principle, anarchists. In reality the Christians' expectation of the End is the hope for a kingdom which comes only from God, not one which men undertake to establish on their own by the destruction of the framework of this present age to which the institution of the State belongs. The consequence of this expectation, therefore, is that this framework is accepted as willed by God, and that within this framework the disciple of Jesus works for the coming Kingdom, thus remaining loyal to the State even though, to be sure, he is in principal critical."[7]

A most fitting remark to this aspect of our study is found in Cullman's advice: "Many a persecution of Christians could have been avoided if the State had taken the pains to understand their attitude and to convince itself of their loyalty. The cross of Christ in itself should remind all responsible statesmen to examine the Christians' real attitude toward the State."[8]

On the pragmatic level very few people have, in our own time, sought more intensely for the proper understanding of the relationship between the two kingdoms than Charles Colson. The quest grew out of his life-experience. For four years he served as special counsel to President Richard M. Nixon. Having pleaded guilty to charges related to the Watergate case, he was imprisoned. After his release from prison he established Prison Fellowship, the largest prison outreach in history. In 1992 he received the Templeton Prize for Progress in Religion, given annually to a person who has advanced humankind's understanding of God. We will make reference to a few key statements from his book Kingdoms In Conflict. Colson confesses that he, like the Jews at the time of Christ and most people since, thought of the kingdom of God as other kingdoms, namely, metaphorically "as geographic entities, physical realms with boundaries and defenses and treasuries." He then states, "But the kingdom of God is a rule, not a realm. It is the declaration of God's absolute sovereignty, of His total order of life in this world and the next."[9]

Having pointed out that the two stages of the kingdom of God (as reflected in the events of the first and second coming of Christ) are often misunderstood, Colson writes: "Many soldiers died to bring about victory in Europe. But in the kingdom of God, it was the death of the king that assured the victory. And this leads to a third reason that the kingdom is often misunderstood: the nature

of the King Himself." Accordingly, "The church, while not the
kingdom of God, is to live out the values of the Kingdom of God
in this world, resisting the ever-present temptation to usher in the
Kingdom of God by political means. Yet this is the temptation to
which the church has most commonly succumbed, and certainly
this is its greatest temptation today." [10]

THE JURISDICTION OF THE TWO KINGDOMS

In the early church (of the Acts of the Apostles and the Epistles) we find illustrations of the extent of the power, authority,
rights, and control given by God to the two kingdoms. The resurrection and ascension of Christ as well as the experience of
Pentecost opened the eyes of the disciples to perceive correctly
the notion of the kingdom of Christ including the issue of church-
state relationship. The theocracy of the Pharisees and Zealots and
the political submissiveness to the Roman state by the Sadducees
were replaced by the primitive church in the message and application of Christ's kingdom. The disciples did what Christ had done,
"proclaiming the gospel of the Kingdom" (Matt. 4:23). When the
people responded to the apostles' message, we are told, "the high
priest rose up, along with his associates (that is, the rest of the
Sadducees), and they were filled with jealousy; and they laid hands
on the apostles, and put them in a public jail." They were brought
"before the Council. And the high priest questioned them, saying,
We gave you strict orders not to continue teaching in this name,
and behold, you have filled Jerusalem with your teaching." The
answer Peter and the apostles gave expressed a foundational religious right and freedom: "We must obey God rather than man"
(Acts 5:17–18). Christ, Himself, had said: "But seek first His kingdom and His righteousness" (Matt. 6:33). This is the first "freedom for."

As a moral being the individual is free to decide his own destiny but is accountable to God. Eventually he must "appear before
the judgment seat of Christ" and "be recompensed for his deeds
in the body, according to what he has done, whether good or bad"

(2 Cor. 5:10). The same is the case with the nations at large. God "made from one, every nation of mankind to live on all the face of the earth, having determined their appointed times, and the boundaries of their habitation" (Acts 17:26). King Nebuchadnezzar was brought before the judgment seat of God. He was deprived of his kingship and was told by the prophet Daniel, "Seven periods of time will pass over you, until you recognize that the Most High is ruler over the realm of mankind, and bestows it on whomever He wishes" (Dan. 4:25).

The intended legitimate sphere of authority and jurisdiction given by God to the civil rules is that of protecting the rights of people and punishing transgressions. Accordingly, the Christian should have a positive attitude to civil authorities. The prophet Jeremiah wrote to the Jewish captives in Babylon: "Seek the welfare of the city where I have sent you into exile, and pray to the Lord on its behalf; for in its welfare you will have welfare" (Jer. 29:7). The apostle Paul expressed himself to the same effect (see 1 Tim 2:1–2; Titus 3:1); likewise the apostle Peter encouraged Christ's followers: "Submit yourselves for the Lord's sake to every human institution, whether to a king as to one in authority, or to governors as sent by him for the punishment of evildoers and the praise of those who do right" (1 Peter 2:13–14). Having stated that "every person be in subjection to the governing authorities," the apostle Paul outlined the positive relationship between the Christians and the civil authorities (Rom. 13:2–7).

The relationship we are dealing with was in a most practical way illustrated in Paul's own experience. In the city of Corinth Paul preached the gospel for about a year and a half. He was opposed by the Jews who brought him before Gallio, the Roman proconsul. An accusation was brought against Paul: "This man persuades men to worship God contrary to the law." Sitting on his judgment seat the Roman proconsul said: "If it were a matter of wrong or of vicious crime, O Jews, it would be reasonable for me to put up with you; but if there are questions about words and names and your law, look after it yourselves; I am unwilling to be a judge of these matters" (Acts 18:13–15). As a representative of state authority Gallio could not have expressed its jurisdiction more clearly: when it comes to civil wrong doings I will judge, but not when it comes to religious issues. Accordingly, we are told that he dismissed the Jews "from the judgment seat."

When Paul came to Ephesus he had to face a conflict with the city's pagan religion and its guild of silversmiths "who made silver shrines of Artemis." A riot started and they cried out, "Great is Artemis of the Ephesians!" The town clerk intervened, arguing that Paul and his associates were neither robbers or blasphemers. He found no real reason for riot and if they brought the case to the court they would "be unable to account for this disorderly gathering." Having said that, "he dismissed the assembly" (Acts 19:23– 41).

In the closing chapters of the Acts of the Apostles, we find recorded Paul's meetings with Felix and Festus, the Roman governors. Paul appealed to his Roman citizenship in order to seek the protection of the state. When some Jews in Jerusalem had decided to kill Paul, the chief captain arranged that 200 solders, 70 horsemen, and 200 spearmen should bring Paul safely to the governor, who resided in Caesarea (Acts 23:15– 25). The various hearings, which Paul had, clearly tell us that Roman authorities exercised only civil authority and found Paul innocent. The opportunity, which the various hearings gave Paul to witness, is of great significance. Finally, Paul placed his case in the hands of the Caesar. He declared: "I have committed no offense either against the Law of the Jews or against the temple or against Caesar.... I am standing before Caesar's tribunal, where I ought to be tried. I have done no wrong to the Jews, as you also very well know. If then I am a wrongdoer, and have committed anything worthy of death, I do not refuse to die; but if none of those things is true of which these men accuse me, no one can hand me over to them. I appeal to Caesar" (Acts 25:8, 10– 11).

Paul was sent to Rome, but about the court case in Rome we are not informed. The Acts of the Apostles closes by telling us that Paul "stayed two full years in his own rented quarters, and was welcoming all who came to him, preaching the kingdom of God,

and teaching concerning the Lord Jesus Christ with all openness"
(Acts 28:30, 31).

During the decades prior to Nero, Rome protected the primitive church from being destroyed by its opponents whether Jews
or gentiles. The church, on the other hand, concentrated on the
proclamation of the gospel in an eschatological setting and did
not interfere with the political affairs of the state. In a nutshell
we have here the historical beginning of religious freedom in the
Christian era. Further, to a large degree this counts for the rapid
growth of Christianity. Paul tells the Colossians that the gospel
"has come to you, just as in all the world also" (Col. 1:6).

It will be most appropriate to close with the conclusion written
by the historian Philip Schaff in his work The Progress of Religious Freedom. Schaff writes: "The Church needs and should ask
nothing from the State but the protection of law. She commends
herself best to the world by attending to her proper spiritual duties
and keeping aloof from political and secular complications. She
can only lose by force and violence; she can only gain and succeed
by the spiritual weapons of truth and love. The whole solution of
the problem of the relation of Church and State lies in the declaration of Christ: 'My kingdom is not of this world'; and in that
wisest answer ever given to a perplexing question: 'Render unto
Caesar the things that are Caesar's, and unto God the things that
are God's.' "[11]

IV

Church-State Relations: A European Survey

The history of Christendom is to a large degree a story of a constant interaction, counteraction, or collision between church and state. The principles, concepts, and forces at play—negatively and positively—in this struggle are still at work for better or worse. The vigilance, which is required to preserve freedom of conscience and religious liberty as well as separation of church and state, necessitates a clear awareness of the historical roots. Accordingly, we will attempt to deal with historical roots within a bird's-eye view of church history, so that in the light of history we may better be able to evaluate the present and hopefully make the right choices for the future.[1]

THE CONSTANTINIAN STATE-CHURCH

We have already observed that the primitive church was pro-tected by the Roman state and that during this period church and state kept their jurisdiction within their own sphere. Beginning with Nero and until the time of Constantine we find ten major persecutions of the Christians caused by the required emperor worship in which the Christians could not participate.

A new phase of church-state relationships began when the emperors Constantine and Licinius issued the Edict of Milan, A.D. 313, granting Christians and non-Christians religious freedom. We will let the Edict speak for itself: "We therefore announce that, notwithstanding any provisions concerning the Christians in our former instructions, all who choose that religion are to be per-mitted to continue therein, without any let or hindrance, and are not to be in any way troubled or molested. Note that at the same time all others are to be allowed the free and unrestricted practice of their religions; for it accords with good order of the realm and the peacefulness of our times that each should have freedom to worship God after his own choice, and we do not intend to detract from the honor due to any religion or its followers."[2]

This edict opened the door for freedom of conscience and religion. Unfortunately, there gradually developed a civil jurisdic-tion of the affairs of the church which made indistinct the bound-aries between church and state.

Christianity gradually assumed a favored status as Constan-tine through lawgiving showed favor to the Christian clergy and church. In Constantine's mind Christianity was the bond that could cement divisive elements of the empire. The empire "had one Emperor, one law, and one citizenship for all free men. It should have one religion."[3] Decisive authority under the new con-ditions was the emperor. "Councils of the church passed upon questions of creed and of organization, but it remained with the imperial authorities to confirm and execute the anathemas against recurring heresy or the decisions as to conflicting claims of power and precedence. For good or for evil the church was in politics."[4]

Having declared himself a Christian, Constantine's aim was to unite the secular state with the Christian church by the closest ties possible. He himself generously supported the church and its clergy with money, buildings, and property. Great as were the favors that Constantine showed to the church, "they were only for that strong, close-knit, hierarchically organized portion that called itself the 'Catholic.' The various 'heretical' sects—and they were still many—could look for no bounty from his hands."[5] In other words, the imperial state church, built upon the supportive decrees of the state, became an intolerant church.

Emperor Constantine's recognition of the church and its subsequent association with the Roman state strongly influenced the practical organization of the church, which was made to conform to the civil organization of the empire. As Christianity spread, a bishop was appointed over each city and the territory attached to it. "The power and prestige of the clergy—the Christian ordo—increased as...the bishop became the most important figure in the life of the city and the representative of the whole community."[6] The move of the capital to Constantinople became an advantage to the bishop of Rome. No longer overshadowed by the emperor, he took over "vacated imperial prerogatives; it left him, for long periods, remaining symbol and source of authority."[7]

At the time of the Protestant Reformation of the 16th century, those who advocated separation of church and state considered the Constantinian state-church, as it developed, a great apostasy, whereas those who adhered to a unified state-church concept saw the Constantinian period as the beginning of the golden age of the church.

EMPEROR JUSTINIAN'S LAWGIVING

During the reign of Emperor Justinian I (A.D. 527– 565) the Roman Empire was once more united. We are told that "Justinian, like Constantine, exercised the right to legislate for every phase of church life. His theory was that 'human and divine authority,' that is civic and ecclesiastical law, 'combining in one and the same act,' formed 'one true and perfect law for all.' " Further, "He meant to exercise a spiritual power very much like the temporal power he wielded.... The jurisdiction of the clergy was clearly defined and minutely regulated as an extension of civil power. In all cases the Emperor was the court of final decision."[8]

Justinian codified the Roman law and incorporated ecclesiastical laws in his Corpus Juris Romani. In this way ecclesiastical laws were enforced by civil authority. Justinian issued severe laws against heretics that is, those who were not in harmony with the bishop of Rome. Heretics, decreed Justinian, "might not hold public office, engage in the liberal professions, hold meetings or maintain churches of their own, or even enjoy all the civil rights of the Roman citizen: for them, said Justinian, 'to exist is sufficient.' "[9] The medieval church taught Justinian's Code to the barbarian nations of Europe. Central and Northern Europe were christianized to a large degree through the enforcement of Justinian's Corpus Juris Romani. During the Protestant Reformation the Reformers used the laws of Justinian to justify persecution and capital punishment of Anabaptists and Anti-Trinitarians.

In the year A.D. 533 Justinian issued a most significant decree concerning papal supremacy: "Therefore we have been diligent both in subjecting and uniting unto your holiness all the clergy of the entire region of the East; ...and it is our firm resolve never to permit any matter touching the general state of the Church to be stirred, however manifest and free from doubt such matters may be, without notifying the same to your holiness, who are the head of all the holy churches; thus in all things striving to increase the honour and authority of your see."[10]

Accepting this decree in its most literal sense, Pope John II (A.D. 533– 535) wrote: "Preserving the reverence due the Roman see, you have subjected all things unto her, and reduced all churches to that unity which dwelleth in her alone, to whom the Lord, through the prince of the apostles, did delegate all power;... and that the apostolic see is in verity the head of all churches, both the rules of the fathers and statutes of the princes do manifestly declare, and the same is now witnessed by your imperial piety."[11]

When the pope stated that the emperor had "reduced all churches to that unity which dwelleth in her alone," and the Roman see "is in verity the head of all churches," he expressed and defined Roman Catholic ecumenism even of the latter part of the twentieth century.

THE GROWING SUPREMACY OF THE CHURCH
The breakdown of the Roman Empire and the rapid spread of Christianity finally led to a situation in which the bishop of Rome, now head of the Western Church, had at times more prestige and power than the kings. Thus it was that in "the Middle Ages the Church was not a State, it was the State; the State or rather the civil authority (for a separate society was not recognized), was merely the police department of the Church." Historian John N. Figgis continues by saying that the church "took over from the Roman Empire its theory of the absolute and universal jurisdiction of the supreme authority."[12]

The image of the pope was also enhanced by the coronation of Charlemagne on Christmas Day of the year A.D. 800. The general impression of the coronation that remained in the mind of the succeeding generation was the picture of the pope placing the crown on the head of a kneeling king. "Such a sight as that of an emperor being crowned by a Pope had never been seen before. The basilica of St. Peter was henceforth regarded as the cradle of the empire, which owed its rebirth to the Apostolic Vicar, the Pope."[13]

The medieval church became a most powerful political institution. The sword was used for the church and by its direction. This is illustrated by the Crusades (1096– 1270), which transferred the leadership of Europe from the emperor to the pope.[14]

PAPAL SUPREMACY
Between 1073 and 1302 the papacy attained its maximum medieval power.

Pope Gregory VII (1073– 1085)

This pope summed up his conception of the pope in a document entitled Dictatus Papae. This document makes the pope God's representative on earth with absolute power over the church and secular rulers. It contains 27 short propositions. We will list a few of these: "The pope can be judged by no one; the Roman church has never erred and never will err till the end of time;...he [the pope] alone can call general councils and authorize canon law; he alone can revise his own judgments; he alone can use the imperial insignia; he can depose emperors; he can absolve subjects from their allegiance."[15] These assertions "comprise a complete programme of action. They imply nothing less than a total papal sovereignty in all affairs of the Christian community."[16]

Pope Innocent II (1198– 1216).

On various occasions in the history of the church we find the title "Vicar of Christ" used with reference to the bishops, but Innocent II claimed the title exclusively for himself, as holder of the unique chair of St. Peter. Philip Schaff points out Innocent's concept of universal sovereignty: "The pope is the vicar of Christ, yea of God himself. Not only is he intrusted with the Dominion of the Church, but also with the rule of the whole world. Like Melchizedek, he is at once king and priest. All things in heaven and earth and in hell are subject to Christ. So are they also to his vicar."[17]

Pope Boniface VIII (1294– 1303).

The highest claim for ecclesiastical power was expressed by Boniface VIII when he concluded the bull Unam Sanctum by saying: "We declare, state, define, and pronounce that it is altogether necessary to salvation for every human creature to be subject to the Roman pontiff." Boniface makes it unmistakably clear that "two swords, the spiritual and the temporal...are in the power of the church." He repeats: "Both are in the power of the Church, the spiritual sword and the material. But the latter is to be used for the Church, the former by her; the former by the priest, the latter by kings and captains but at the will and by the permission of the priest. The one sword, then, should be under the other, and temporal authority subject to spiritual." He further states: "If, therefore, the earthly power err, it shall be judged by the spiritual power; and if a lesser power err, it shall be judged by a greater. But if the supreme power err, it can only be judged by God, not by man."[18]

Climaxing centuries of persistent papal claims for supremacy, Boniface VIII placed the capstone on medieval ecclesiastical structure of universal jurisdiction.

Thomas Aquinas (c. 1225– 1275).

The claims of Boniface VIII had been prepared theologically by Thomas Aquinas, who is considered the theologian of the Roman Catholic Church. Thomas Aquinas had made the papal claim of supremacy an integral part of Catholic theology: "As for the Church itself, Rome is the mistress and mother of all churches. To obey her is to obey Christ. This is according to the decision of the holy councils and the holy Fathers. The unity of the Church presupposes a supreme centre of authority. To the pope, it belongs to determine what is of faith. Yea, subjection to him is necessary to salvation."[19]

Aquinas also says that "the secular power is joined to the spiritual, as in the pope, who holds the apex of both authorities, the spiritual and the secular."[20] Theologian Reinhold Seeberg writes regarding Aquinas' political theory: "The church attains its summit in the pope. With Aristotle, it was held: 'But the best government of a multitude is that it be ruled by one.' "[21]

Ecclesiastical Law-giving.

Canon law is a collection of ecclesiastical decretals and regulations that express the norm for the life of the individual Christian as well as the church collectively. Boniface VIII combined all the past decretals with his own numerous bulls into a single collection. Issued in 1298 under the name Liber Sextus, it included the bull Unam Sanctam. With some additions and revisions, the canonical collection Liber Sextus remained the fundamental canon law until the twentieth century.

A complete overhaul of canon law resulted in a new collection of canon law and decretals in 1917. It was comprised of 2414 canons. When, in 1959, Pope John XIII announced his plan to summon the second Vatican Council, he also made known that he intended to establish a commission to revise the 1917 code of canon law in order to update it with the decrees to be promulgated by the forthcoming council. On January 25, 1983, Pope John Paul II made an official declaration regarding acceptance of the new and revised code of canon law. For the purpose of the present study it is sufficient to state that no Roman Catholic doctrine has been altered; likewise, the concept of papal supremacy remains the same.

The past conflict between Roman Catholic canon law and civil law and jurisdiction remains with us today. In whatever form the issues may appear, the basic fact remains that canon law was and is "the scientific expression of the papal power of universal jurisdiction."[22]

PRECURSORS OF A NEW ORDER

The tragic history of the papacy after the pontificate of Boniface VIII testifies to the fact that the papal claim for universal supremacy became its Achilles' heel. Boniface VIII died as a captive in the Vatican. Then followed the Babylonian Captivity of the popes (1309– 1377), when the popes resided in Avignon in France as absentee landlords of the papal states. During the Papal Schism (1378– 1417) two lines of popes, one residing in Rome and the other in Avignon, competed for the loyalty of Europe. The Council of Constance (1414– 1417) healed the schism but burned Hus at the stake and ordered the bones of Wiclif burned.

The waning of the influence of the Roman hierarchy and its structure made possible new advances in religious experience and thinking as well as in science. We think of Copernicus and Galileo in the field of astronomy, and Lorenzo Valla and Nicholas of Cusa in linguistic and historical studies. In comparing the Latin Vulgate with the Greek New Testament, Valla demonstrated the many inadequacies of the former. New religious experience in the life of the individual was reflected in lay piety and new devotional literature. One example is Thomas a Kempis' Imitation of Christ.

We now turn to two "thinkers" who created philosophical, theological, and political concepts which have remained with us to the present.

Marsilius of Padua (c. 1275– 1342).

In the ongoing struggle between pope and emperor, between church and state, a new note was sounded by Marsilius "a thinker whose influence, though greater after his death than in his lifetime, was that of a portent."[23] His book, Defensor Pacis, set forth most of the ideas which were to become "the creative forces of the modern era." He has been characterized as "a precursor of the Reformation, a theorist of popular sovereignty and constitutional systems, a herald of the modern sovereign state."[24] He "arrived at the fully matured principle of religious toleration."[25] According to M. Emerton, former professor of Ecclesiastical History at Harvard University, "His book has often been called the most remarkable literary product of the Middle Ages, and I am inclined to accept this verdict." He was "the herald of a new world, the prophet of a new social order."[26]

The aim of Defensor Pacis is to explain "the principal causes whereby civil peace or tranquility exists and is preserved, and whereby the opposed strife arises and is checked and destroyed."[27] The one singular cause which Marsilius sets forth as the root of strife and the hindrance of peace is "the belief, desire, and undertaking whereby the Roman bishop and his clerical coterie, in particular, are aiming to seize secular rulerships and to possess excessive temporal wealth."[28]

Marsilius rejects the idea that the sovereignty of the state rests with "a certain few" rather than with "the whole body of citizens or the weightier multitude thereof."[29] The same principle is also the basis for his structure of the church. According to Marsilius, "the truest and the most fitting" meaning of the word "church" is "the whole body of the faithful who believe in and invoke the name of Christ, and all the parts of this whole body in any community, even the household."[30]

Marsilius' basic principle, that the source of all power is the people, became the constitutive principle for the modern democratic states. Accordingly, one of the authorities on the political ideas of Marsilius writes; "The permanent significance of Marsilius' ideas is to be found not merely in his opposition to the papal and ecclesiastic institutions of medieval Christendom, but in the entire doctrinal structure which he adduces in support of such opposition."[31]

William of Occam (c. 1290– 1349).

Like Marsilius, William of Occam taught that the philosopher and theologian must begin with the individual. Stephen C. Tornay, an authority on the philosophy of Occam, writes that Occam thus "presents a strong evaluation of the human personality as against the corporate political body, reflecting Occam's emphasis on the concrete and individual in his theory of knowledge as against the general and universal."[32]

Occam strongly emphasized that the apostolic principle, which should be followed by the pope and the bishops, is that of serving the church spiritually.[33] Since the clergy should not be occupied with secular matters, Occam encourages the idea that laymen care for secular business connected with the administration of the church.[34]

Characteristic is Occam's constant appeal to Scripture as the final source of authority. No doctrine not rooted in Holy Scripture should be acknowledged as catholic and necessary to salvation. In the introduction to his last treatise he wrote: "Yet let all men hold this as certain: that in matters of faith and of knowledge, one evident reason or one authority of Scripture reasonably understood will move me more than the assertion of the whole world of mortal men...."[35]

Occam was a distant voice of the Protestant Reformation; no wonder Luther called him "my dear Master," and said "I am of the Occamist faction." Occam "stands in a direct relation to the greatest event of the succeeding age, the Reformation.... He was no forerunner for Luther as a Reformer; but he was one of the factors without which the Reformation would have been impossible."[36]

Marsilius' and Occam's ideas influenced John Wyclif (c. 1327–1384) and John Hus (c. 1369– 1415) to become reformers. Both advocated the doctrine of the priesthood of believers and became the morning stars of the Protestant Reformation. In the light of what we have observed, it is understandable that Luther, with the other Protestant Reformers, had to re-evaluate the concept of the church.

LUTHER'S CHURCH-STATE RELATIONS

Luther began his reformatory activities by proclaiming the doctrine of sola fide (by faith alone), which called for a reformation of the church, and its relationship to the state, as anticipated by the theories of Marsilius and Occam. It has been pointed out that "it was Luther who accomplished the true deliverance of the State; he achieved it by removing the differentiation between ecclesiastically good works and worldly activities and by limiting religion and the Church to their proper sphere." Further, the "decision which lay in the final elimination of all claims of sovereignty of the Church over the State was the victory of modern State whose sovereignty could already be proclaimed at the end of the sixteenth century. Luther brought about this decision."[37]

On the basis of Christ's words, "Render to Caesar the things that are Caesar's; and to God the things that are God's" (Matt. 22:21), Luther made a sharp distinction between church and state: "God has ordained two governments among the children of Adam,—the reign of God under Christ, and the reign of the world under the civil magistrate, each with its own laws and rights. The laws of the reign of the world extend no further than body and goods and the external affairs on earth. But over the soul God can and will allow no one to rule but himself alone. Therefore where the worldly government dares to give laws to the soul, it invades the reign of God, and only seduces and corrupts the soul."[38] The church historian Philip Schaff called this statement by Luther "a prophetic anticipation of the American separation of church and state."[39]

For a time Luther conceived of the church as a voluntary group of committed Christians, but he later changed his concept. For political reasons he placed the church under the general supervision of the state. The price Luther paid for the help of the territorial princes was high. Karl Holl, a defender of Luther, admits that the "best energies of the Reformation were kept down through this development or they were forced to develop alongside and apart from the Church."[40] An outstanding American Lutheran scholar, the late Professor J. L. Neve, has said that the establishment of Lutheran territorial churches "laid the foundation for a continuing injury to Lutheranism from which Germany is suffering to this present day."[41]

The Lutheran state church became a persecuting church. At the Diet of Worms in 1521 Luther championed religious liberty when he said, "To act against our conscience is neither safe of us nor open to us. On this I take my stand. I can do no other. God help me. Amen." During the early years of the Reformation he made many statements affirming religious liberty,[42] but in later years, when facing his opponents, Luther displayed a spirit of intolerance and harshness toward those who differed from him. This is evident with respect to Baptists, Roman Catholics, and Jews alike. His intimate associate, the otherwise mild Melanchthon, wrote about the Baptists in 1530: "I am now of the opinion that persons who defend an article of doctrine which, though not insurrectory, is openly blasphemous should be put to death by the authorities, for these must punish open blasphemy as much as other public crimes. The law of Moses teaches us this."[43]

CALVIN'S CHURCH-STATE RELATIONS

In his Institutes of the Christian Religion Calvin emphasizes that God in His Word declares, "By me kings reign, and rulers decree justice" (Prov. 8:15), and "there is no authority except from God, and those which exist are established by God" (Rom. 13:1).[44] Calvin advocates the duty of nonresistance,[45] but emphatically states that a person ought not obey magistrates if it means disobeying God. He sought to transform the civil government of Geneva into harmony with the Law of God, thus making the magistrates real servants of the Lord. When and where that was not accomplished, he left the way open for political resistance.

Calvin was greatly opposed to any interference by the civil powers in the internal affairs of the church, but his idea that Christ should govern the magistrates tied the state to the church in what may be styled a theocracy or bibliocracy. This form of government also led to intolerance in Geneva itself and later among the Puritans in New England. Philip Schaff writes: "The union of church and state accounts for the persecution of papists, heretics, and Jews; and all the Reformers justified persecution to the extent of deposition and exile, some even to the extent of death, as in the case of Servetus. The modern progress of the principle of toleration and religious liberty goes hand in hand with the loosening of the bond of union between church and state."[46]

In his theocratic concept Calvin was closer to Rome than was Luther, but in his Presbyterian form of church organization, he gave a significance to the individual "which of necessity leads to a democratic conception and development of the entire ecclesiastical system."[47] In the various councils in Geneva, laymen, teachers, and ministers decided together on disciplinary matters. Calvin also gave to the local congregation a voice in the choice of its officers. Nevertheless, it was only with the Presbyterian and congregational forms of church government in a society with absolute separation of church and state, that religious liberty could develop.

RELIGIOUS LIBERTY IN FRANCE

Some of the darkest pages in the history of toleration and religious liberty were written in France. The Huguenots, as Protestants were called in France, suffered more than any of the major Protestant groups. The horrible massacre of St. Bartholomew's Day in 1572 when, during a royal wedding, thousands upon thousands of Protestants were tortured or killed, is only one instance of what had been going on almost constantly on a small scale for nearly half a century.

In spite of the massacre of St. Bartholomew, more and more Frenchmen embraced the Protestant faith and in 1598 the Edict of Nantes was issued. It recognized the liberty of private conscience, but although it restricted the liberty of public worship, it nevertheless stands among the great monuments of the European quest for freedom. Effectiveness of the provisions of the Edict of Nantes depended almost entirely on the will of the ruling monarch. One by one the privileges of the Protestants were abridged, and their condition became gradually more and more intolerable until the revocation of the Edict of Nantes by Louis XIV in 1685. This edict ordered all Protestant churches and private schools destroyed. The Huguenots were forbidden to gather for religious services; their children were to be baptized by a Catholic priest and brought up as Catholics. The Edict of Revocation was followed through to the bitter end with utmost vigor. The prisons were filled with Huguenots and a large number were tortured to death. The number who left France were in the hundreds of thousands. They were among the ablest, wealthiest, and most enterprising Frenchmen. These events are considered some of the darkest days in the history of France and the history of religious freedom.

The quest for liberty during the second half of the eighteenth century manifested itself in the writings of men as Voltaire who "advocated toleration as a right of justice, a duty of humanity, a condition of the prosperity of the State, and as the only basis of peace between the State and religion, and the different religions. Toleration promotes population. It alone makes society endurable. The Christian religion, he thought, ought to be the most tolerant, because Christians have been the most intolerant among men."[48]

In its Constitution of the year 1793 the Revolutionary Government stated in Article VII: "The right to express one's thoughts and opinions by means of the press or in any other manner, the right to assemble peaceably, the free pursuit of religion, cannot be forbidden."[49] The thought of this Article is similar to that of the First Amendment of the American Constitution.

It is significant that 1260 years after Emperor Justinian had made the bishop of Rome the head of all Christendom, and thus the custodian of Roman and canon law in the West, France abolished the canon law, took the pope into captivity, and established the free exercise of religion. The verdict of history made the decision inevitable.

RELIGIOUS LIBERTY IN ENGLAND

During the Reformation period the ruling monarch was the supreme authority in the English Church. Henry VIII (1509–1547) persecuted Protestant dissenters and Roman Catholics alike, depending on his changing moods. During the reign of his Protestant son, Edward VI (1547–1553), persecution practically ceased, but under Queen Mary (1553–1558) the Protestants suffered severe martyrdom. The Religious Settlement of Queen Elizabeth (1558–1603) did not include either Puritans or Roman Catholics. James I (1603–1625) and Charles I (1615–1649) followed the line laid down by Queen Elizabeth, but the Puritan forces of opposition that had developed during her reign grew ever stronger as the civil and ecclesiastical administration became more and more despotic.

After the execution of Charles I in 1649, Cromwell gave to the major Evangelical groups equality to the extent that they were not suspected of disloyalty. Congregationalists, Presbyterian, and

Evangelical churchmen were eligible to become ministers in the parish churches, but Catholics and Unitarians were excluded. Following the temporary triumph of the Independents under Cromwell and the Commonwealth (1649– 1660) came the reactionary reigns of Charles II and James II. Charles II (1660– 1685) renewed the Elizabethan Act of Uniformity and passed several intolerant laws against dissenters with the result that more than 2,000 Presbyterian, Congregational, and Baptist ministers were driven from their churches.

Finally, during the reign of King James II (1685– 1688) the nation revolted against the despotism of its last two kings and brought William of Orange to the English throne. (He was married to a sister of James II.) He was disposed to tolerate differences of religious opinion, and in 1689, four years after Louis XIV had revoked the Edict of Nantes, he issued his Edict of Toleration. Its significance has been summarized as follows: "The Act of Toleration left the Church of England unchanged, and in possession of all her endowments, rights, and privileges, but it limited her jurisdiction, so that she ceased from that time on to be coextensive with the nation. It gave the orthodox Protestant Dissenters, under certain conditions and restrictions, a legal existence, and the right of public worship and self-government, dependent upon self-support (for these two are inseparably connected). Its benefit extended to Presbyterians, Independents, Baptists, and Quakers, but to no others."[50]

THE RADICAL REFORMATION

In the past, historians spoke only about the Reformation initiated by the Protestant Reformers and the opposition to it by the Roman Catholics in the Counter-Reformation. Now it is recognized that there was a third and equally important movement: the Radical Reformation developed by the Anabaptists. George H. Williams, while at Harvard Divinity School, contributed greatly to the recovery of this fact. He says: "The Radical Reformation was a tremendous movement at the core of Christendom.... It was as much an entity as the Reformation itself and the Counter Reformation."[51]

The Anabaptists were firm in their rejection of an alliance between church and state. Their concept of the church as a voluntary congregation did not harmonize with the view that the church was identical with the people at large in a given territory. Further, the Anabaptists refused to let the problem of a possible survival influence their commitment to remain separate from the state. All believers were part of the priesthood of believers and in their self-governing congregations their "voices" were equally heard. This had a great influence upon the formation of democratic principles. In this connection it should be noticed that A. D. Lindsay in The Modern Democratic State claims: "The most significant thing about Puritan democratic theory is that the Puritans began with the experience of working a small and thoroughly democratic society, the Puritan congregation. Their idea of a church is that it is a fellowship of active believers. The Puritans of the Left, with whom democratic theories mostly originated, were all congregationalists."[52]

In the Netherlands, which had a representative form of government, the Baptists found a place of refuge. It has been pointed out that the "Reformation in the Netherlands from 1530 to 1566 is known to have been practically nothing else than the history of the Baptist churches in that country, the significance of this movement is apparent. Modern democracy, as has often been pointed out,…has in a large degree sprung from the labors of the Dutch Baptists and their associates in England, who followed them much later."[53]

During the persecution of dissenters in England many fled to the Netherlands, where they found a haven of refuge. These refugees, whether Independents or Calvinists, were strongly influenced by the democratic principles of the Anabaptists and the Dutch people, and for a time Cromwell considered uniting his own commonwealth with that of the Dutch. We have already noticed that the inner religious struggle in England ended in the

Act of Toleration of 1689, which William of Orange issued soon after he became king of England.

SUMMARY

The historical survey of European church-state relationships points out three key systems, which were incompatible and therefore in conflict, one with the other. We meet the three systems already in the New Testament. The one was promoted by Christ and the apostolic church; the other two systems were adhered to, respectively, by the Pharisees and the Sadducees. The first had a theological and Christological foundation for religious freedom and took a firm stand for separation of church and state in which each kept jurisdiction within its own sphere. On the contrary, the Pharisees believed in a theocracy while the Sadducees were subservient to the Roman authorities.

In spite of persecution the early ancient church remained faithful to the ideals of the New Testament. Beginning with Constantine, a new phase of church-state relationship began. Religious freedom was granted to Christians and non-Christians. However, the emperor's involvement with the church resulted in a growing linkage between church and state.

A close tie between church and state remained throughout the Middle Ages. During certain periods the state had distinct jurisdiction over the church. At other times the church exercised supremacy over the state, specifically in form of the Papacy. In fact, the medieval church became a most powerful political institution.

During the Reformation of the 16th century the three different church-state concepts were illustrated anew. In the beginning of the Reformation in the 16th century Luther advocated freedom of conscience and declared that church and state were two different spheres of existence. However, for various reasons Luther accepted the assistance of the state, and from this linkage developed a state-church.

Calvin, unlike Luther, was opposed to any interference by the secular authorities in the church's internal affairs, but on the other hand he tied the state to the church in such a way that the magistrates were under the jurisdiction of the church. This form of theocracy became the model for the followers of Calvin.

The Reformation in England separated the church from the supremacy of the pope, but made the monarch the "single and supreme Lord" or "supreme head" of the Church of England. Those who felt that the English Reformation did not go far enough were name Puritans. To a large degree they were Calvinists, holding Calvin's church-state concept. In their ecclesiology Anglicans and Puritans, each in their own way, linked together church and state.

It is understandable that the Anabaptist groups which developed outside the Lutheran and Calvinistic churches felt strongly—as the harmful results of alliance between church and state became apparent—that outward separation from the state-church was an inward liberation from the influences of the theological principles and unbiblical ecclesiasticism of the Middle Ages, which the Protestant Reformation sought to undo. The Anabaptists sought not merely a reformation of the church but a restitution of the New Testament church. This quest resulted in a renewal of religious freedom and the refusing of synergism between church and state.

V

The American Development of a Free Church in a Free State

During the Colonial period the American religious life was shaped by the various forms of Protestant Christianity which the immigrants brought with them from Europe. Among them we find the three main systems of church-state relationship manifested in a marked way with the related issues of freedom of conscience and religion .

Virginia approved the state-church concept. Massachusetts adhered to the theocratic idea and Rhode Island implemented separation of church and state from the very beginning. The other colonies followed, with more or less variations, one of the three patterns.

The European conflicts regarding the value and implementation of one of the three systems continued in American. In Europe no universal agreement was ever reached, but in America the Colonial period closed with a general unanimity. The latter is one of the most noteworthy and consequential facts of history, and its story we will briefly trace.

THE STATE-CHURCH OF VIRGINIA

The first permanent English colony in American was James-town, Virginia. The charter was issued in April 1606 and the first Colonists settled in the following spring. The charter issued by King James had a religious overtone. It expressed the desire and hope for a work which would "by the Providence of Almighty God, hereafter tend to the glory of his Divine Majesty, in propa-gating of Christian-Religion to such People, as yet living in Dark-ness and miserable Ignorance of the true Knowledge and Worship of god...."[1]

In November 1906, the Articles, Instructions and Orders was issued. It clearly indicated that the religious instruction should be in harmony with the Church of England. The Document asserted: "And wee doe specially ordaine, charge, and require, the said presidents and councells, and the ministers of the said several col-onies respectively, within their several limits and precincts, that they, with all diligence, care, and respect, doe provide, that the true word, and service of God and Christian faith be preached, planted and used not only within every of the said several colonies, and plantations, but alsoe as much as they may amongst the sal-vage people, which doe or shall adjoine unto them, or border upon them, according to the doctrine, rights, and religion now professed and established within our realme of England...."[2]

In the first three charters (1606, 1609, 1612) King James I introduced himself as the Defender of the Faith. He closed the second charter by stating, "And lastly, because the principal Effect which we can desire or expect of this Action, is the Conversion and Reduction of the People on those Parts unto the true Worship of God and Christian Religion, in which Respect we should be loath that any Person should be permitted to pass that we sus-pected to affect the Superstitions of the Church of Rome, we do hereby DECLARE, that it is our Will and Pleasure that none be permitted to pass in any Voyage from Time to Time to be made into the said Country, but such as first shall have taken the Oath of Supremacy; For which Purpose, we do by these Presents give full Power and Authority to the Treasurer for the Time being, and any three of the Council, to tender and exhibit the said Oath, to all such Persons as shall at any Time be sent and employed in the said Voyage."[3] It is obvious that the oath to be taken was intended to eliminate any nonconformist.

In 1611 Thomas Dale became governor. He was expected, among other things, to improve the moral and religious condition of the colony; for this purpose he issued Laws Divine, Moral and Martial. The section on religion tells us:

1. To speak impiously of the Trinity or one of the Divine Persons, or gainst the known articles of Christian faith, was punishable with death.

2. The same penalty of death was to avenge "blaspheming God's holy Name."

3. To curse of "banne"—for the first offence some severe punishment; for the second a "bodkin should be thrust through the tongue"; if the culprit was incorrigible, he should suffer death.

4. To say or do anything "to the derision or despight of God's holy word'" or in disrespect to any Minister, exposed the offender to be "openly whipt 3 times, and to ask public forgiveness in the assembly of the congregation, 3 several Saboth daies."

5. Non-attendance on religious services entailed a penalty, for the first offence, of the stoppage of allowance; for the second, whipping; for the third, the galleys for six months.

6. For Sabbath-breaking the first offence brought the stoppage of allowance; the second, whipping; and the third, death.

7. Preachers and ministers were enjoined to faithfulness in the conduct of regular services on pain "of losing their entertainment."

8. Every person in the colony, or who should come into it, was required to repair to the Minister for examination in the faith. If he should be unsound, he was to be instructed. If any refused to go to the minister, he should be whipt; on a second refusal he should be whipt twice and compelled to "acknowledge his fault on Saboth day in the assembly of the congregation"; for a third refusal he should be "whipt every day until he makes acknowledgement."[4]

While the extreme punishments were not implemented, the document still reveals what the governor considered legitimate within the state-church system.

The mental and religious attitudes nourished by the state-church concept resulted in the enactment of various religious laws, though less severe.

The law of 1623–24, regarding church attendance, read: "Whosoever shall absent himself from divine service any Sunday, without an allowable excuse, shall forfeit a pound of tobacco, and he that absenteth himself a month shall forfeit 50 lbs. of tobacco."[5]

A law demanding baptism of children was issued in 1662: "Whereas many schismatical persons, out of their adverseness to the orthodox established religion, or out of the new-fangled conceits of their own heretical inventions, refuse to have their children baptized; be it, therefore, enacted, by the authority aforesaid, that all persons that, in contempt of the divine sacrament of baptism, shall refuse, when they may carry their child [children] to a lawful minister in that county to have them baptized, shall be amerced two thousand pounds of tobacco, half to the informer, half to the public."[6]

Also in 1662 a law was issued forbidding travel on Sunday: "Enacted that the Lord's Day be kept holy, and no journeys be made on that day unless upon necessity. And all persons inhabiting

in this country having no lawful excuse, shall every Sunday resort
to the parish church or chappel, and there abide orderly during
the common prayer, preaching, and divine service, upon the penalty of being fined 50 lbs. of Tobacco by the County Court."[7]

A specific law against the Quakers was enforced in 1663:
"If any Quakers, or other Separatists whatsoever in this colony,
assemble themselves together to the number of 5 of more, of the
age of 16 years, or upwards, under the pretence of joyning in a
Religious worship not authorized in England or this country, the
parties so offending, being thereof lawfully convicted by verdict,
confessions, or notorious evidence of the fact, shall for the first
offence forfeit and pay 200 lbs. of Tobacco; for the second offence
500 lbs. of Tobacco, to be levied by warrant from any Justice of the
Peace, upon the goods of the party convicted; but if he be unable,
then upon the goods of any other of the Separatists or Quakers
then present. And for the third offence, the offender being convicted as aforesaid, shall be banisht the colony of Virginia."[8]

Other laws and regulations were passed: "Fines were imposed
for nonattendance at church service, and payment of tithes was
made compulsory on all and a first lien on every resident's tobacco.
Besides the tithes, every parson was entitled to a piece of land,
called the glebe. Parish churches were built by local taxation, and
all ministers had to 'conform themselves in all things according to
the canons of the Church of England.' "[9]

The Church of England remained by law the state-church of
Virginia until 1776, when a new constitution was enacted. This will
be considered later, and we will then find an opposite concept of
church-state relationship from what we have observed thus far.

Having dealt with the Church of England, it should be noticed
that the Carolinas established the Church of England in 1706
(South) and 1715 (North). In Maryland, which was founded as a
Roman Catholic colony with religious freedom, Protestants gradually outnumbered the Catholics. In 1691 the colony was annexed
by England and the Anglican Church was established by law.

THE THEOCRACY OF MASSACHUSETTS

In England the religious settlement of Queen Elizabeth did not include the Puritans. Their opposition grew during the reign of her successors and reached a breaking point when King Charles I appointed William Laud as bishop of London, 1628, and five years later as archbishop of Canterbury. In a strong way Laud enforced the observance of conformation to the Thirty-nine Articles of the Church of England with the result that the Puritan preachers, mainly being Calvinists in theology and ecclesiology, were silenced. Being denied the opportunity of freely living their own religious life the Puritans sought their freedom by emigrating to Massachusetts. The freedom they sought was for themselves and was not extended to others.

In 1628 the emigration to Massachusetts began and the next year the royal charter was obtained. It should be noticed that the charter did not refer either to religious matters or to religious freedom "for a twofold reason: the crown would not have granted it, and it was not what the grantees wanted. They preferred to keep in their own hands the question as to how much, or how little, religious liberty they should claim or allow."[10]

The charter gave the Puritans an opportunity for self-government which they made full use of in their implementation of a bibliocracy or theocracy: the civil government should put into effect the dictates of the Bible and the church.

The members of the General Court (the legislature of the colony) had to adhere to the Puritan faith. Thus it was hoped to establish an ideal Christian society, but it was a society only for "the religious right."

The civil government was to be built on the basis of a divine government. In 1623 it was suggested that laws were drafted "agreeable to the word of God...as near to the law of God as they can"[11] and "according to the rule of God's word."[12] One commentator writes: "The General Court of the Massachusetts Bay Colony re-enacted the entire Mosaic code of religious, political, and sanitary laws in the hope of re-establishing the ancient theocracy in the New World, ignorant of the fact that God Himself abolished the theocracy at the time of the Babylonian captivity and decreed that it should not be re-established 'until He come whose right it is; and I will give it Him.' Eze. 21:26, 27. This mistaken conception that the kingdom of God is to be set up again upon earth through human legislation and that the obligations men owe to God are to be enforced by the civil magistrates, has been the primary cause of all the religious persecutions of the past."[13]

In the light of the foregoing it is not surprising that banishment for heresy was implemented. We read from a law of 1646: "It is therefore Ordered and declared by the Court. That if any Christian within this Jurisdiction, shall go about to subvert and destroy the Christian Faith and Religion, by broaching and maintaining any Damnable Heresies: as denying the immortality of the soul, or resurrection of the body, or any sin to be repented of in the regenerate, or any evil done by the outward man to be accounted sin, or denying that Christ gave Himself a ransom for our sins, or shall affirm that we are not justified by His death and righteousness, but by the perfections of our own works, or shall deny the morality of the Fourth Commandment, or shall openly Condemn or oppose the Baptizing of Infants, or shall purposely depart the Congregation at the administration of the Ordinance, or shall deny the ordinance of Magistracy, or their Lawful Authority to make war, or to punish the outward breaches of the first Table, or shall endeavor to seduce others to any of the errors of heresies above mentioned, every such person continuing obstinate therein after due means of Conviction, shall be sentenced to Banishment."[14]

A special law was issued against the Quakers which required death or banishment.[15] In 1659 three Quakers were hanged because of their faith.[16]

Regarding Catholics it was asserted that they could be "Banned on Penalty of Death."[17]

A series of laws were issued regarding church attendance and forbidding labor, sport, and travel on Sunday, since Sunday was considered as the Sabbath. The transgressors were fined, put to servile work or set in cage or stock.[18]

Among the colonies that shared the bibliocracy of Massachusetts, we find "Plymouth, New Haven, Connecticut, and New
Hampshire, with their Congregational Establishments. Among
these it will be observed that theocratic Massachusetts and New
Haven were more closely akin in the strictness of their religious
requirements; that Plymouth and Connecticut were more liberal
in spirit and enactments; while New Hampshire was organized so
long after the period of severity had waned that it furnishes few
illustrations of our theme."[19]

RHODE ISLAND:
SEPARATION OF CHURCH AND STATE

The diametrical contrast between Massachusetts and Rhode
Island is seen in the experience and views of Roger Williams,
1604– 83. He was educated at Cambridge University and came to
Massachusetts during the winter of 1630– 31. He was invited to
minister to the church in Boston but declined because of the close
relationship between church and state. He objected to the civil
government's jurisdiction in matters of conscience, and its punishment for non-authorized religious beliefs or lack of them. For
these reasons Williams continued to oppose the Puritan administration with the result that in October of 1635 the Massachusetts
General Court sentenced Williams to banishment with the understanding of sending him back to England. The court record reads:
"Whereas Mr. Roger Williams, one of the elders of the Church
at Salem, hath broached and divulged divers new and dangerous
opinions, against the authority of magistrates, as also writ letters
of defamation, both of the magistrates and churches here, and
that before any conviction, and yet maintaineth the same without
any retraction; it is therefore ordered that the said Mr. Williams
shall depart out of this jurisdiction within six weeks now next ensu-
ing, which, if he neglect to perform it, it shall be lawful for the
governor and two of the magistrates to send him to some place out
of this jurisdiction, not to return any more without written license
from the Court."[20]

Williams fled and found refuge among the Indians. The following spring he purchased land from the Indians and founded the settlement of Providence, Rhode Island; here he established the first Baptist Church in America. The settlers adopted a covenant, 1638, and a Plantation Agreement, 1640. The new government was legally organized the following year as "a Democracie or Popular Government."[21]

In the meantime Williams made his greatest contribution in molding the thinking of Rhode Island by his booklet The Bloody Tenant of Persecution for the Cause of Conscience. It was written in 1644 and has been described as "an epoch-making milestone in the history of separation of Church and State and of religious freedom."[22] It prepared the way for the work of James Madison and Thomas Jefferson and others a century and a half later.

In the summary of Bloody Tenant twelve principals are listed. We will quote most of these:

"First, That the blood of so many hundred thousand soules of Protestant and Papists, spilt in the Wars of present and former Ages, for their respective Consciences, is not required nor accepted by Jesus Christ the Prince of Peace.

"Fifthly, All Civill States with their Officers of justice in their respective constitutions and administrations are proved essentially Civill, and therefore not Judges, Governours or Defendours of the Spirituall or Christian State and Worship.

"Sixthly, It is the will and command of God, that (since the comming of his Sonne the Lord Jesus) a permission of the most Paganish, Jewish, Turkish, or Antichristian consciences and worships, bee granted to all men in all Nations and Countries: and they are onely to bee fought against with that Sword which is only (in soule matters) able to conquer, to wit, the Sword of Gods Spirit, the Word of God.

"Seventhly, The State of the Land of Israel, the Kings and people thereof in Peace & War, is proved figurative and ceremoniall, and no patterne nor president for any Kingdome or civill State in the world to follow.

"Eighthly, God requireth not an uniformity of Religion to be inacted and inforced in any civill State; which inforced uniformity (sooner or later) is the greatest occasion of civill Warre, ravishing of conscience, persecution of Christ Jesus in his servants, and of the hypocrisie and destruction of millions of souls.

"Tenthly, An inforced uniformity of Religion throughout a Nation or civill State, confounds the Civill and Religious, denies the principles of Christianity and civility, and that Jesus Christ is come in the Flesh.

"Twelfthly, lastly, true civility and Christianity may both flourish in a state or Kingdome, notwithstanding the permission of divers and contrary consciences, either of Jew or Gentile."[23]

In a letter to the town of Providence, 1654, Williams compared the commonwealth to a ship with all different types of passengers: "That ever I should speak or write a tittle, that tends to such an infinite liberty of conscience, is a mistake, and which I have ever disclaimed and abhorred. To prevent such mistakes, I shall at present only propose this case: There goes many a ship to sea, with many hundred souls in one ship, whose weal and woe is common, and is a true picture of a commonwealth, or a human combination or society. It hath fallen out sometimes, that both papists and protestants, Jews and Turks, may be embarked in one ship; upon which supposal I affirm, that all the liberty of conscience, that ever I pleaded for, turns upon these two hinges—that none of the papists, protestants, Jews, or Turks, be forced to come to the ship's prayers or worship, nor compelled from their own particular prayers or worship, if they practice any."[24]

Roger Williams and his colleague John Clarke had worked untiringly to obtain a charter that would unite Rhode Island and Providence. Such a one was granted by King Charles II in 1663. The Charter of Rhode Island and Providence Plantation was considered as an experiment and unique when compared with others. The king writes in the opening pages of the charter: "And whereas, in theire humble address, they have freely declared, that it is much on their hearts (if they may be permitted), to hold forth a livlie experiment, that a most flourishing civil state may stand and best bee maintained, and that among our English subjects, with a full libertie in religious concernements.... That our royall will and pleasure is, that noe person within the sayd colonye, at any tyme hereafter, shall bee any wise molested, punished, disquieted, or called in question, for any differences in opinione in matters of religion."[25]

In the renown work The Rise of Religious Liberty in America, Sanford H. Cobb makes the following comment on the charter: "Thus was constituted, and by a king whose tendencies and desires were all toward despotism, a genuine republic—the first thoroughly free government in the world, where the state was left plastic to the moulding will of the citizen; the conscience at liberty to express itself in any way of doctrine and worship; the Church untrammelled by any prescription or preference of the civil law. In this little colony of Rhode Island was first set up this 'ensign for the people,' the model for that sisterhood of states which was yet to possess the continent." Cobb closes his comments by stating: "With such a beginning the further history of religious liberty in Rhode Island presents little matter for comment. The battle was already won, the colony started at the point which the most of her sisters reached only at the Revolution."[26]

The colonies which in ideology came close to Rhode Island were Pennsylvania and Delaware. Neither had a state church and freedom was granted to believers in God.

RELIGIOUS FREEDOM IN THE STATE CONSTITUTIONS OF THE REVOLUTION

We observed in the previous paragraph that in regard to religious freedom, Rhode Island began where the other states did not begin until the time of the Revolution. It is the latter we wish to observe. Prior to the Constitution of the United States with its Bill of Rights, most of the states enacted new local constitutions; in these religious liberty and freedom of conscience were endorsed. These constitutions tell us that the various states wished to begin the United States of America on the same democratic basis and the same foundation for religious freedom as did Rhode Island. We will quote the provisions made in several of these constitutions beginning with Virginia and Massachusetts.

Constitution of Virginia - 1776: "Section 1. That all men are by nature equally free and independent, and have certain inherent rights, of which, when they enter into a state of society, they cannot, by any compact, deprive or divest their posterity; namely, the enjoyment of life and liberty, with the means of acquiring and possessing property, and pursuing and obtaining happiness and safety. Sec. 16. That religion, or the duty which we owe to our Creator, and the manner of discharging it, can be directed only by reason and conviction, not by force or violence; and therefore all men are equally entitled to the free exercise of religion, according to the dictates of conscience; and that it is the mutual duty of all to practise Christian forbearance, love, and charity towards each other."[27]

Constitution of Massachusetts - 1780: "Article I. All men are born free and equal, and have certain natural, essential, and unalienable rights; among which may be reckoned the right of enjoying and defending their lives and liberties; that of acquiring, possessing, and protecting property; in fine, that of seeking and obtaining their safety and happiness. II. It is the right as well as the duty of all men in society, publicly and at stated seasons, to worship the SUPREME BEING, the great Creator and Preserver of the Universe. And no subject shall be hurt, molested, or restrained, in his person, liberty, or estate, for worshipping God in the manner and season most agreeable to the dictates of his own conscience; or for his religious profession of sentiments; provided he doth not disturb the public peace, or obstruct others in their religious worship."[28]

Constitution of North Carolina - 1776: "XIX. That all men have a natural and unalienable right to worship Almighty God according to the dictates of their own consciences."[29]

Constitution of Pennsylvania - 1776: "II. That all men have a natural and unalienable right to worship Almighty God according to the dictates of their own consciences and understanding:

And that no man ought or of right can be compelled to attend any religious worship, or erect or support any place of worship, or maintain any ministry, contrary to, or against, his own free will and consent: Nor can any man, who acknowledges the being of a God, be just deprived or abridged of any civil right as a citizen, on account of his religious sentiments or peculiar mode of religious worship; And that no authority can or ought to be vested in, or assumed by any power whatever, that shall in any case interfere with, or in any manner controul, the right of conscience in the free exercise of religious worship."[30]

The other states expressed themselves in terms similar to the four which have been cited. Rhode Island did not feel the need of a new constitution but published one in 1842. It is interesting to notice a statement in the preamble of the new constitution: "We, the people of the State of Rhode Island and Providence Plantations, grateful to Almighty God for the civil and religious liberty which He hath so long permitted us to enjoy, and looking to him for a blessing upon our endeavors to secure and to transmit the same unimpaired to succeeding generations, do ordain and establish this constitution of government."[31]

Connecticut adopted a constitution in 1818. Section 3 and 4 of Article One relates to religious freedom: "Sec. 3. The exercise and enjoyment of religious profession and worship, without discrimination, shall forever be free to all persons in this State, provided that the right hereby declared and established shall not be so construed as to excuse acts of licentiousness, or to justify practices inconsistent with the peace and safety of the State. Sec. 4. No preference shall be given by law to any Christian sect or mode of worship."[32]

JAMES MADISON'S MEMORIAL AND REMONSTRANCE

During the Revolution and the formative years of the United States the influence of James Madison was of paramount significance. He was a Roger Williams of his time, championing for full religious liberty and freedom of conscience. The Virginia Constitution of 1776 was drawn up by George Mason and in the original draft the section on religion read "that all men should enjoy the fullest toleration in the exercise of religion." Madison objected to the word "toleration" for it contrived "dangerous implications." He explained: "Toleration belonged to a system where was an established Church, and where a certain liberty of worship was granted, not of right, but of grace; while the interposition of the magistrate might annul the grant." Mason's draft, which referred to "toleration" was substituted by the sentence, "all men are equally entitled to the free exercise of religion, according to the dictates of conscience." Regarding this change under the influence of Madison, one historian writes: "Thus the definition of the Virginia Bill of Rights took took final shape, expressing the best concept of religious liberty that had as yet found outside of Rhode Island."[33]

However, the struggle and process of the disestablishment of the church in Virginia continued. The arguments for and against establishment of the church included the payment of tithes and the support of the church and its ministry. In 1784 the Assembly of Virginia presented a bill which required all citizens "to pay a moderate tax or contribution annually for the support of the Christian religion, or of some Christian church, denomination or communion of Christians, or for some form of Christian worship." In the preamble the motivation for passing this bill was that "the general diffusion of Christian knowledge hath a natural tendency to correct the morals of men, restrain their vices, and preserve the peace of society; which cannot be effected without a competent provision for licensed teachings...." Quoting this bill Leo Pfeffer makes this comment: "The preamble is of great significance, because it recognized the widely held belief that religion was not within the competence of civil legislatures. It sought to justify intervention not on any theocratic ground but on what today would be called the 'police' or 'welfare' power. Government support of religion is required to restrain vice and preserve peace, not to promote God's kingdom on earth."[34]

The opposition to the bill got the voting of the bill postponed. In the meantime Madison wrote the Memorial, which furnishes fifteen sections giving reasons why religion did not come within the sphere of the civil government. Part of Section 1. reads: "The Religion then of every man must be left to the conviction and conscience of every man; and it is the right of every man to exercise it as these may dictate. This right is in its nature an unalienable right.... We maintain therefore that in matters of religion, no man's right is abridged by the institution of Civil Society, and that Religion is wholly exempt from its cognizance."[35]

In Section 8. Madison asks and answers two pertinent questions: "If religion be not within the cognizance of Civil Government, how can its legal establishment be necessary to civil government? What influence in fact have ecclesiastical establishments had on Civil Society? In some instances they have been seen to erect a spiritual tyranny on the ruins of civil authority: in many instances they have been seen upholding the thrones of political tyranny: in no instance have they been seen the guardians of the liberties of the people."[36]

The arguments presented in the Memorial created a strong resentment against the proposed assessment bill and it was overthrown. The Memorial itself remains as "one of the most important and eloquent documents in the history of the achievement of religious liberty and the separation of church and state in the United States."[37]

THOMAS JEFFERSON'S BILL FOR ESTABLISHING RELIGIOUS FREEDOM

The successful results of Madison's Memorial in defeating the Virginia assessment bill encouraged Madison and others to clinch the victory by bringing forward, as a bill, a declaration on religious freedom written by Thomas Jefferson. It had been written back in 1777 and presented to the Virginia Assembly in 1779 but laid aside until it was presented in the fall of 1785 and finally signed as a bill in January 1786 with the title An Act Establishing Religious Freedom.

The first and major part of the bill serves as a preamble and gives the reason why the document should be accepted. One historian has summarized it with six short propositions:

1. God made man's mind free, and deliberately chose that religion should be propagated by reason and not by coercion.

2. Legislators and rulers have impiously assumed dominion over faith, and have established and maintained false religions.

3. It is sinful and tyrannical to compel a man to furnish contributions for the propagation of opinions which he disbelieves and abhors; and it is also wrong to force him to support this or that teacher of his own religious persuasion.

4. Our civil rights have no dependence on our religious opinion, and therefore imposing religious qualifications for civil office tends to corrupt religion by bribery to obtain purely external conformity.

5. The opinions of men are not the object of civil government, nor under its jurisdiction. It is a dangerous fallacy to restrain the profession of opinions because of their ill tendency; it is enough for the rightful purpose of Civil Government for its officers to interfere when principles break into overt acts against peace and good order.

6. Truth is great and will prevail if left to herself. Truth has nothing to fear from the conflict with error.[38]

The central part of the bill reads: "Be it therefore enacted by the General Assembly, that no man shall be compelled to support any religious worship, place, or ministry whatsoever; nor shall be forced, restrained, molested, or burthened in his body or goods, nor shall otherwise suffer, on account of his religious opinions or belief. But that all men shall be free to profess, and by argument to maintain, their opinion in matters of religion; and that the small shall in no wise diminish, enlarge, or affect their civil capacities." The closing paragraph stipulates, "that the rights hereby asserted, are natural rights of mankind; and that if any act shall be hereafter passed to repeal the present or to narrow its operation, such act will be in infringement of natural right."[39]

The three writings by Roger Williams, James Madison, and Thomas Jefferson prepared, both philosophically and by their practical implementation, the way for the United States Constitution and its Bill of Rights.

THE U.S. CONSTITUTION AND ITS AMENDMENTS

The Constitutional Convention composed of fifty-five men representing the various states, met in Philadelphia during the summer of 1787 and drafted the Constitution, which was voted by the Continental Congress the same year. Both the House and the Senate voted the Bill of Rights in the fall of 1789 and by 1791 it was ratified by the various states. Together the two documents are the capstone of the quest and development of religious freedom and church-state separation as we have traced it.

In view of the fact that those who drafted the Constitution believed in the separation of church and state caused them to write a secular document which constituted the principles for a civil government. No allusion is made to God. The only reference it makes to religion is the closing sentence of Article VI, which states that "no religious test shall ever be required as a qualification to any office or public trust under the United States."[40] The very nature of the document is embedded in the proposition that church and state shall be separate.

Robert L. Maddox writes: "In fact, they drafted a document that provided for a government that was neutral when it came to religion. The country and the people could be as religious as it/ they chose, but the government as government would maintain a stance of appreciative neutrality toward religion and religions."[41]

The Bill of Rights further substantiates what has been said about the Constitution. Only the first article refers to religion, pointing out that freedom of religion is the first freedom: "Congress shall make no law respecting an establishment of religion, or prohibiting the free exercise thereof, or abridging the freedom of speech, or of the press; or the right of the people peaceably to assemble, and to petition the Government for a redress of grievances."[42]

In his work Church and State in the United States A. P. Stokes makes the following valuable comment: "These rights are interrelated. They are all of importance from the standpoint of the Churches. Freedom of speech is related to preaching; freedom of the press to religious journalism; freedom of assembly and petition to church meetings."[43]

The same year as George Washington became president, 1789, he wrote a letter to the United Baptist Churches of Virginia. It leaves no doubt regarding his understanding of the Constitution's approval of religious liberty and freedom of conscience: "If I could have entertained the slightest apprehension, that the constitution framed in the convention, where I had the honor to preside, might possibly endanger the religious rights of any ecclesiastical society, certainly I would never have placed my signature to it.... If I could conceive that the general government might ever be so administered as to render the liberty of conscience insecure, I beg you will be persuaded, that no one would be more zealous than myself to establish effectual barriers against the horror of spiritual tyranny, and every species of religious persecution."[44]

In 1802, the year after he became president, Thomas Jefferson wrote a letter to the Danbury Baptists of Connecticut in which the wall of separation between church and state is used to explain the practical application of the Constitution's endorsement of religious freedom. Jefferson wrote: "Believing with you that religion is a matter which lies solely between man and his God, that he owes account to none other for his faith or his worship, that the legislative powers of government reach actions only, and not opinions, I contemplate with sovereign reverence that act of the whole

American people which declared that their legislature should 'make no law respecting an establishment of religion, or prohibiting the free exercise thereof,' thus building a wall of separation between Church and State."[45]

The Constitution did not merely change the course for church-state relationship from the time of Constantine, but restored for both church and state the New Testament principle of dignity and freedom of man and its teaching regarding two spheres of existence, civil and religious. The result was a free church in a free state, each discharging its respective responsibilities. This is the source of America's greatness and account for its blessings.

Reflecting on the United States Constitution and its significance in the history of church-state relationships, the 19th century renowned British statesman Gladstone said: "The American Constitution is, so far as I can see, the most wonderful work ever struck off at a given time by the brain and purpose of man."[46]

In the next chapter we will observe milestones of religious liberty in the 20th century. These would never have been erected had it not been for the U. S. Constitution and its practical application of religious liberty during two centuries. We will close with a quotation from an American champion of religious liberty and the editor for may years of the magazine, Liberty. In an address in Constitutional Hall, Washington, D. C., 1966, Roland R. Hegstad said: "Our forefathers did not erect the wall of separation because they were irreligious, but because they were religious. They saw the wall of separation as a wall of protection for both church and state...They wrote our Constitution against the backdrop of European church-state conflict that had ravaged the Continent for centuries. It is no wonder that they said, 'Enough of cooperation of church and state; for the sake of both, for the sake of free men, let us have separation.' And so they built a wall..."[47]

VI

Milestones of Religious Freedom in the Twentieth Century

After two world wars, the second half of the 20th Century witnessed an international concern for human rights and religious freedom. The outcome was the drafting and adoption of several documents which have remained landmarks in the quest for religious freedom. The major agencies which took active part were the World Council of Churches, the Second Vatican Council, and the United Nations.

THE WORLD COUNCIL OF CHURCHES
The First Assembly of the World Council of Churches was held in Amsterdam in August 1948. At this conference 147

churches were represented and an official Declaration on Religious Liberty was issued. The making of such a document had been on its way for about a decade. In 1937 the World Conference on Church, Community, and State was held in Oxford, England. In its final report are listed the essential "freedoms" which are necessary for the church in order to fulfill its mission. The same is the case in the Report on Church and State from the Conference of the International Missionary Council, Madras, 1938.[1]

In America the Federal Council of Churches and the Foreign Missions Conference established a Joint Committee on Religious Liberty (1944) from which we quote: "The right of individuals everywhere to religious liberty shall be recognized and, subject only to the maintenance of public order and security, shall be guaranteed against legal provisions and administrative acts which would impose political, economic, or social disabilities on grounds of religion. Religious liberty shall be interpreted to include freedom to worship according to conscience and to bring up children in the faith of their parents; freedom for the individual to change his religion; freedom to preach, educate, publish and carry on missionary activities; and freedom to organise with others, and to acquire and hold property for these purposes."[2]

This Statement on Religious Liberty was sent to President Franklin D. Roosevelt and to the members of the U. S. Government, as well as to State and Church leaders abroad. It had a great impact on the drafting of the United Nations Charter and the World Council of Churches Declaration on Religious Liberty to which we now will turn.

The introduction of the WCC Declaration (1948) states: "The rights of religious freedom herein declared shall be recognized and observed for all persons without distinction as to race, color, sex, language, or religion and without imposition of disabilities by virtue of legal provision of administrative acts." The Declaration as such is composed of four main articles, each containing precise statements and detailed explanations. We will refer to the four basic principles:

1. Every person has the right to determine his own faith and creed.

2. Every person has the right to express his religious belief in worship, teaching, and practice, and to proclaim the implications of his beliefs for relationships in social or political community.

3. Every person has the right to associate with others and to organize with them for religious purposes.

4. Every religious organization, formed or maintained by action in accordance with the rights of individual persons, has the right to determine its policies and practices for the accomplishment of its chosen purposes. (See Appendix One.)

The quest for the application of these principles was taken up at the Second Assembly of the WCC held in 1954 at Evanston, U.S.A. Sorrow was expressed "over the continuing sufferings and disabilities of fellow Christians in many parts of the world." The Assembly made the resolution to reaffirm "previous declarations regarding religious liberty."[3]

The insistence upon the significance of religious freedom continued at the Third Assembly of WCC, New Delhi, 1961, where a second basic instrument on religious liberty was voted by the 577 delegates representing nearly 200 different churches. The New Delhi Statement on Religious Liberty lists very precisely the many "freedoms" which religious liberty necessitates, and introduces the theological and biblical foundation for the same. (See Appendix Two).

In the deliberations and resolutions by the WCC there was no participation by the Roman Catholic Church except the presence of five Roman Catholic observers at the Assembly in New Delhi. However, the WCC no doubt indirectly influenced the Roman Catholic Church. In 1962 the Second Vatican Council was convened and during its various sessions the question of religious freedom was discussed.

THE SECOND VATICAN COUNCIL

After three years of deliberation and re-drafting, Pope Paul VI, on the second to the last day (December 7, 1965) of the Council, promulgated the Declaration on Religious Freedom; its subtitle reads: On The Right of the Person and of Communities to Social and Civil Freedom in Matters Religious. The document is also referred to as the Dignitatis Humanae Personae, which are its opening words in Latin. The opening paragraph reads as follows: "A sense of the dignity of the human person has been impressing itself more and more deeply on the consciousness of contemporary man. And the demand is increasingly made that men should act on their own judgment, enjoying and making use of a responsible freedom.... This demand for freedom in human society chiefly regards the quest for the values proper to the human spirit. It regards, in the first place, the free exercise of religion in society."[4]

By supporting religious freedom the document made the Roman Catholic Church the participant of the general development and appreciation for religious freedom. The document is unique in the sense that it is the first Roman Catholic statement of its kind. Principles expressed are different from those previously promulgated, and this represents a great step forward. Outlining the general principles of religious freedom, the Declaration begins by expressing the following assertions: "This Vatican Synod declares that the human person has a right to religious freedom. This freedom means that all men are to be immune from coercion on the part of individuals or of social groups and of any human powers in such wise that in matters religious no one is to be forced to act in a manner contrary to his own beliefs. Nor is anyone to be restrained from acting in accordance with his own beliefs, whether privately or publicly, whether alone or in association with others, within due limits."[5]

When readers compare the principles which the Declaration lays down as the basis for religious liberty with those of other official statements, they generally agreed that there is a great deal of agreement. However, the Declaration contains loopholes and unexplained utterances. We have already noticed one. The last quoted statement closes with the wording, "within due limits."

Father John Courtney Murray, S.J., of America, was a key person in formulating and promoting the document. He admits that it was "the most controversial document of the whole Council, largely because it raised with sharp emphasis the issue that lay continually below the surface of all the conciliar debates—the issue of the development of doctrine. The notion of development, not the notion of religious freedom, was the real sticking-point for many of those who opposed the Declaration even to the end. The course of the development between the Syllabus of Errors (1864) and Dignitatis Humanae Personae (1965) still remains to be explained by theologians."[6] One of the weak aspects of the document is the lack of this explanation.

The Syllabus of Errors was issued by Pope Pius IX, who presided over the First Vatican Council, 1870, where the teaching of the pontiff was declared infallible. In the Syllabus of Errors the Pope had declared among 80 errors the following principles as errors:

15. Every man is free to embrace and profess the religion he shall believe true, guided by the light of reason.

24. The Church has not the power of availing itself of force, or any direct or indirect power.

55. The Church ought to be separated from the State, and the State from the Church.

78. In the present day, it is no longer expedient that the Catholic religion shall be held as the only religion of the State, to the exclusion of all other modes of worship.[7]

That the Declaration on Religious Freedom was "the most controversial document" of Vatican II is reflected in its somewhat checkered history during the Council and the debates between the conservatives and progressives. When the final vote was taken, 1,954 voted for and 249 against. In view of the fact that the Pope had encouraged the acceptance of the document, the opposition was stronger than the figures indicate. A few statements by the conservatives illustrates some of their objections.

Cardinal Arriba y Castro: "Only the Catholic Church has the duty and the right to preach the Gospel, and therefore proselytism by non-Catholics among Catholics is illicit and must be obstructed not only by the Church but by civil authority itself to the extent the common good requires it."

Cardinal Ruffcini: "As the truth is one, so also the true religion is one, and to it alone properly belongs the right of liberty."

Cardinal Ottaviani: "Truth and falsehood cannot have equal rights The text proposes solutions which are contrary to the common doctrine of the Church."

Cardinal Browne: "Equal rights cannot be given to all religions. The right to spread false doctrine in Catholic countries cannot be given."[8]

The views of the conservatives have been summarized by one of the Anglican observers as follows: "Error has no rights. The Roman Catholic Church alone possesses the truth. Therefore, she demands for herself of the state full religious liberty for her sacred mission. It is the duty of a Catholic state to aid this mission by suppressing other religious groups that disagree with the Catholic Church, for error has not the same rights as truth. The aim of Vatican diplomacy should be to establish this thesis where possible by concordats with Catholic states."[9] Professor William J. Wolf also writes: "It remains to be seen how the 249 opponents will act in the countries in which Roman Catholicism is overwhelmingly dominant and in those in which there are concordats with a confessional state. Will they ignore the Declaration, or will they twist its phrases in a minimalist direction?"[10]

The opening paragraph of the document (which we have already quoted) expresses the great need for religious freedom, but this is followed by reference to true religion: "We believe that this one true religion subsists in the catholic and apostolic church...On their part, all men are bound to seek the truth, especially in what concerns God and His church, and to embrace the truth they came to know, and to hold fast to it." Accordingly, the subject of religious freedom "leaves untouched traditional Catholic doctrine on the moral duty of men and society toward the true religion and toward the one church of Christ."[11]

It has been pointed out that this insertion in an opening statement on religious liberty "gives the unfortunate impression that a Roman Catholic is not free to discuss religious liberty as an issue in itself without talking about the one true Church."[12] In other declarations on religious liberty such misunderstanding is avoided. We will note two examples.

The Second World Congress on Religious Liberty (sponsored by the International Religious Liberty Association and others) had as its theme "Freedom of Religion and Belief: Basis of Peace." The congress, held in Rome in September 1984, was attended by representatives from major religions and political systems who affirmed the theme of the conference. The secretary-general of the International Religious Liberty Association, Bert Beverly Beach, in his welcome and opening remarks stated: "I want freedom for the Christian, Jew, Muslim, Buddhist, and Hindu, old and new religions, for the Marxist and non-Marxist, for the believer and what we call the nonbeliever, for the religious or ideological majority and for the minority. I'll tell you one important reason why: my freedom of conscience and belief is never secure, if your freedom is not secure. I must even guard the freedom of belief of one who might style himself my ideological adversary. Let men travel to their ultimate destiny in freedom and good conscience. Really, freedom of religion allows of no other travel. The spirit of this conference is epitomized in the Golden Rule, which is the concluding statement of the IRLS Declaration of Principles: 'Do unto others as you would have others do unto you.' "[13]

The World Council of Churches New Delhi Declaration clearly states the right of disbelief: "Religious liberty incudes freedom to change one's religion or belief without consequent social, economic, and political disabilities. Implicit in this right is the right freely to maintain one's belief or disbelief without external coercion or disability."[14]

In his comments on the Vatican Declaration on Religious Freedom, Carrillo De Albornoz expresses regret "that the Vatican

Declaration does not expressly proclaim the freedom to change one's religion." He also asks this question: "Does the Declaration recognize the same freedom for non-believing people?" The answer is that "nowhere in the Declaration can there be found an express recognition of this freedom."[15]

Dealing with the liberty of religious groups the question is brought up about the misuse of freedom in evangelism. We read: "In spreading religious faith and in introducing religious practices, everyone ought at all times to refrain from any manner of action which might seem to carry a hint of coercion or of a kind of persuasion that would be dishonorable or unworthy, especially when dealing with poor or uneducated people. Such a manner of action would have to be considered an abuse of one's own right and a violation of the right of others."[16]

Professor William J. Wolf makes this comment: "This is excellent advice and needs to be said, but is there not a danger that a hard-core conservative can find a loophole here? Such a bishop or official of a confessional state might well declare evangelicals guilty in fact of such practice, because of a low level of education among their converts, and as disqualified to continue their activities. The picture of government officials deciding who are and who are not 'rice Christians' is disquieting. One cannot of course provide in advance against every conceivable contingency, but there would seem to be some ground of disquiet here."[17]

With reference to countries when Roman Catholicism is the state religion or has a special preferential position, the Vatican Declaration reads: "If, in view of peculiar circumstances obtaining among certain peoples, special legal recognition is given in the constitutional order of society to one religious body, it is at the same time imperative that the right of all citizens and religious bodies to religious freedom should be recognized and made effective in practice."[18] The positive aspect is, of course, that the minority groups have religious freedom, but it is on a different level than that of the Catholic Church. This means inequality and is not genuine religious freedom. A footnote to this statement explains: "This paragraph is carefully phrased. The Council did not wish to condemn the institution of 'establishment,' the notion of a 'religion of the state.' A respectable opinion maintains that the institution is compatible with full religious freedom."[19]

Regarding religious freedom for the family, we are told that "since the family is a society in its own original right, it has the right freely to live its own domestic religious life under the guidance of parents. Parents, moreover, have the right to determine, in accordance with their own religious beliefs, the kind of religious education that their children are to receive." From this it follows that government "must acknowledge the right of parents to make a genuinely free choice of schools and of other means of education. The use of this freedom of choice is not to be made a reason for imposing unjust burdens on parents, whether directly or indirectly."[20] By stating that the "freedom of choice" in education should not impose "unjust burdens—whether directly or indirectly" the government's duty to support the schools of a church is brought in through a back door.

Whatever weakness may be found in the Vatican's Declaration on Religious Freedom it must be appreciated that in the efforts for the furtherance of religious freedom a Roman Catholic document can now be cited to enforce this essential principle. At the same time it must also be pointed out that Roman Catholics and Protestants may use the same nomenclature when discussing religious freedom, but the concepts may not be identical; and this is understandable, for each operates—philosophically and pragmatically, theologically and ecclesiologically—within a different framework.

It is hoped—and needed—that the "course of the development between the Syllabus of Errors (1864) and Dignitatus Humanae Personae (1965)" which at the time of Vatican II remained "to be explained by the theologians," will finally be explained and thus further clarify the principles and theological concepts undergirding the document's practical applications.

Thinking especially of the American situation it would be worthwhile to keep in mind the words expressed by President John F. Kennedy, a Roman Catholic, to a large group of ministers of the gospel and a television audience of millions in 1960.

Kennedy said, "I believe in an America where the separation of church and state is absolute—where no Catholic prelate would tell the President (should he be Catholic) how to act and no Protestant minister would tell his parishioners for whom to vote—where no church or church school is granted any public funds or political preference—and where no man is denied public office merely because his religion differs from the President who might appoint him or the people who might elect him."[21]

THE UNITED NATIONS

Since its inception after the Second World War, the United Nations has declared religious freedom to be a basic human right. In December 1948, (the same year as the World Council of Churches voted its Declaration on Religious Liberty) the United Nations adopted the Universal Declaration of Human Rights. The document declares itself to be "a common standard of achievement for all peoples and nations."[22]

In the Preamble a number of reasons are given for the acceptance of the Declaration. The first is the "recognition of the inherent dignity and of the equal and inalienable rights of all members of the human family is the foundation of freedom, justice and peace in the world.". Article 1 likewise states the philosophical basis: "All human beings are born free and equal in dignity and rights. They are endowed with reason and conscience and should act towards one another in a spirit of brotherhood."

The rights and freedoms advocated are the rights of everyone "without distinction of any kind, such as race, colour, sex, language, religion" (Article 2). Dealing with marriage Article 16 also refers to religion: "Men and women of full age, without any limitation due to race, nationality or religion, have the right to marry and to found a family."

Religious freedom is directly declared in Article 18: "Everybody has the right to freedom of thought, conscience and religion; this right includes freedom to change his religion or belief, and freedom, either alone or in community with others and in public or private, to manifest his religion or belief in teaching, practice, worship and observance."

The subject of religious liberty and freedom of conscience has continually had a significant place in the resolutions of the United Nations. In 1951 a Convention Relating to the Status of Refugees was adopted. (A "Convention" is a binding treaty for each signatory state.) The Convention was formulated "owing to well-founded fear of being persecuted for race, religion, nationality," etc., and prescribes that the "contracting states shall apply the provisions of this Convention to refugees without discrimination as to race, religion or country of origin" (Article 3). Article 4 deals directly with religion: "Contracting states shall accord to stateless persons within their territories treatment at least as favourable as that accorded to their nationals with respect to freedom to practise their religion and freedom as regards the religious education of their children."[23]

When we turn to the Convention Relating to the Status of Stateless Persons (1954) we find the same provision as made for refugees.[24] In the International Convention On the Elimination of All Forms of Racial Discriminations (1965) it was re-emphasized that the U.N. was established "to promote and encourage universal respect for and observance of human rights and fundamental freedoms for all, without distinction as to race, sex, language or religion."[25] Regarding freedom of religion the International Covenant On Civil and Political Rights (1966) restates Article 18 of the Universal Declaration of Human Rights and adds three brief amplifications.[26]

The United Nations Charter was drafted in 1945 at the San Francisco Conference. At that time some countries and "representatives of forty-two United States non-governmental organizations, argued strenuously for the inclusion in the Charter of precise, detailed provisions for the protection of the freedom of thought, conscience and religion."[27] We have observed that the Charter of 1948 did not give a "detailed provision" for religious freedom. However, the goal was not lost sight of.

After more than three decades of study and consultations, the General Assembly of the United Nations accepted, in 1981, a detailed Declaration On the Elimination of All Forms of Intolerance and Discrimination Based on Religion or Belief.[28] The document contains eight articles and most of them have one or more subdivisions. (The articles have a preamble of seven "considerations" and "convictions"; one of them reads: "Considering that religion or belief be fully respected and guaranteed,..." The preamble closes with the resolution "to adopt all necessary measures for the speedy elimination of such intolerance in all its forms and manifestations and to prevent and combat discrimination on the grounds of religion or belief."

The first four Articles emphasize in greater detail what previous UN religious freedom statements convey. Article 5 deals with parents and their children's religious education. The Article stipulates: "The parents or, as the case may be, the legal guardians of the child have the right to organize the life within the family in accordance with their religion or belief and bearing in mind the moral education in which they believe the child should be brought up." Further, "The child shall be protected from any form of discrimination on the grounds of religion or belief. He shall be brought up in a spirit of understanding, tolerance, friendship among peoples, peace and universal brotherhood, respect for freedom of religion or belief of others, and in full consciousness that his energy and talents should be devoted to the service of his fellow men."

Nine "freedoms" are included in "the right to freedom of thought, conscience, religion or belief" (Article 6). They are listed as follows:

(a) To worship or assemble in connection with a religion or belief, and to establish and maintain places for these purposes;

(b) To establish and maintain appropriate charitable or humanitarian institutions;

(c) To make, acquire and use to an adequate extent the necessary articles and materials related to the rites or customs of a religion or belief;

(d) To write, issue and disseminate relevant publications in these areas;

(e) To teach a religion or belief in places suitable for these purposes;

(f) To solicit and receive voluntary financial and other contributions from individuals and institutions;

(g) To train, appoint, elect or designate by succession appropriate leaders called for by the requirements and standards of any religion or belief;

(h) To observe days of rest and to celebrate holidays and ceremonies in accordance with the precepts of one's religion or belief;

(i) To establish and maintain communications with individuals and communities in matters of religion or belief at the national and international levels.

Next, the document stipulates that the "rights and freedoms set forth in the present Declaration shall be accorded in national legislation in such a manner that everyone shall be able to avail himself of such rights and freedoms in practice."

Among the nine freedoms listed above, the one which deals with freedom "to observe days of rest" is rather unique and new in an international document. Its significance requires a few observations. When the Roman Emperor Constantine, who considered himself Pontific Maximus, issued the first Sunday law, stipulating "rest upon the venerable day of the sun," he became—in the words of the church historian, Philip Schaff—"the founder, in part at least, of civil observance of Sunday." It should be noticed that Constantine "enjoined the observance, or rather forbade the public desecration of Sunday, not under the name of Sabbatum or Dies Domini, but under its old astrological and heathen title, Dies Solis, familiar to all his subjects, so that the law was as applicable to the worshippers of Hercules, Apollo and Mithras, as to the Christians. There is no reference whatever in his law either to the fourth commandment or to the resurrection of Christ."[29]

Sunday legislation was continued by Constantine's successors. In 386 the Roman legislation used for the first time the term "Lord's Day" as a synonym for "the day of the sun."[30] The union of church and state has its beginning with Constantine, and from then on Sunday legislation has been a prominent or distinct "mark" of that union, ignoring that the biblical day of rest is the Sabbath, the seventh day of the week.

After the decline of the Roman Empire, the church-councils enacted Sunday laws and during the Middle Ages their enforcement was theocratic in nature. The Protestant Reformation of the 16th century retained close ties with the state, and Sunday legislation continued.

The Puritans in England, especially during Cromwell, emphasized that Sunday was not merely celebrated as a memorial of Christ's resurrection, but the sacredness of the Sabbath (the 7th day of the week) of the Ten Commandments was transferred to Sunday. This concept augmented the theocratic nature of Sunday legislation. In America during the Colonial period Sunday legislation was greatly influenced by the Puritan Sabbath concept. Those who desecrated the Sabbath (Sunday) by work, play, travel, etc., or abstained from church services were fined or placed in the stocks.

After the Colonial period the Sunday laws were modified, but they created an anomaly. The United States Constitution with its First Amendment stipulated that church and state are free from interference one from the other. However, various states continued separately to enact Sunday laws. Referring to this inconsistency, one historian writes: "The inconsistency revealed in many cases is most striking. That the lawmakers must have had some questions in their minds concerning their right to legislate on purely religious matters is shown by the fact that in many States exemptions from the provisions of the Sunday laws are made for those who conscientiously observe another day than Sunday."[31]

During the 19th century debates for and against Sunday laws were often vigorous, but in the latter part of the 20th century it appears that Sunday laws are "dead letter" in those states which still retain them on paper.

Having given an overview of the history of blue laws (Sunday Laws) one impartial author concludes: "Almost from their earliest inception and for most of their history, blue laws have been closely and explicitly tied to the church. The separation of church and state mandated by the U. S. Constitution has, over the past two centuries, eliminated much of the overt religious support for Sunday-closing laws.... Instead, the states, for a variety of reasons... insisted upon the right to regulate Sunday trading for secular reasons." It should also be noticed that dealing with "the demise of blue laws" in the United States, the same author informs us that "in 1970, twenty-five states had statewide blue laws, with enforcement of varying intensity. By 1984, twelve of these states had repealed their Sunday-closing legislation, and others were threatening to modify or repeal their respective restrictions."[32] However, as long as some states have not repealed their local Sunday laws, vigilance is required regarding church-state separation. The same vigilance is specifically required if some should encourage civil authorities to support Sunday legislation for religious reasons.

In 1991 the present pope, John Paul II, issued an encyclical challenging the civil governments to consider "Sunday as a day of rest; calling the position a 'human right, which is based on a commandment.' " Pope John Paul II has specifically encouraged the member states of the European Economic Community to enact Sunday laws for religious reasons.[33] In America religious right organizations and Roman Catholic bishops are no doubt in sympathy or agreement with John Paul II. Pat Robertson in his book The New World Order strongly advocates that Sunday should be observed as the biblical Sabbath of the Ten Commandments.[34]

When the state of Massachusetts sought to liberalize its Sunday-closing legislation, 1991, its governor was strongly opposed by Bernard Law, a Roman Catholic cardinal. Said the cardinal: "...our governor chooses to diminish in this Commonwealth what little remains of a governmental recognition of the Sabbath. In the Christian tradition we are reminded that man was not made for the Sabbath, the Sabbath was made for man."[35]

It should be kept in mind that those countries which have legalized Sunday rest do not have a better church attendance or religious and moral life than does the United States; the contrary is rather the case. The spiritual and transforming power of the Kingdom of God—working through the church—is not ushered in by governmental regulations but by an existence where church and state recognize their respective spheres of jurisdiction also when it comes to the implementation of the freedom "to observe days of rest...in accordance with the principles of one's religion or belief."

In the beginning of the Second World War President Franklin D. Roosevelt, 1941, erected a monument for human rights and religious liberty when he stated his four freedoms: freedom of speech; freedom of every person to worship God in his own way; freedom from want; and freedom from fear—everywhere in the world. We have briefly traced the development of the freedom of religion, but the latter cannot be separated from the other three as it is rather the foundation for them.

We have observed that the second half of the 20th century has provided international instruments which should give guarantee to, and can be quoted for, the furtherance of religious freedom. The significance of practicing religious freedom has been made indisputably clear; likewise, it is obvious that if religious freedom is not adhered to, then the future will bring trouble and disaster both for church and state. Realization of religious freedom also means that it will be possible for the gospel of Christ to be "preached in the whole world for a witness to all nations" (Matt. 24:14).

Epilogue, by B. B. Beach

Religious Freedom Facing the Third Millennium

SOME FUNDAMENTAL POSITIVE FACTS

Religious liberty is on the move often for better and sometimes for worse. As we approach the third millennium, we can be grateful for several important and fundamental facts. Increasing numbers of people are benefitting from gradual or dramatically rapid advances in human rights, especially freedom of religion.

First of all, since 1948, the year of the Universal Declaration of Human Rights, there is reasonably strong United nations backing expressed in international documents which categorically affirm freedom of conscience and belief, as well as liberty of religious practice, as integral elements of modern society.

Secondly, since 1948, the World Council of Churches has supported these ideas, even to the extent of having a religious liberty secretariat. Although the secretariat was closed for financial reasons, the WCC maintains a staff that takes a special interest in religious liberty issues. And there is a secretariat dealing with International Affairs, Peace and Human Rights.

A third, and in many ways astonishing, factor is the official espousal of religious liberty by the Roman Catholic Church. This was manifested in 1965 when the Second Vatican Council adopted a ground-breaking Declaration supporting religious liberty in civil society. The Council strongly affirmed that in principle no one is to be restricted in his or her religious beliefs and practices. Since then, numerous papal statements have upheld religious liberty, including freedom of religion for minorities where there is a dominant or established church. Certain Catholic countries, which once persecuted or discriminated against non-Catholics, now practice religious liberty. The first two articles of the 1993 Fundamental Agreement between the Holy See and the State of Israel deal with freedom of religion and conscience. The changed situation needs to be watched, assessed, and constantly re-evaluated.

A fourth positive factor is the collapse of totalitarian Communism in Eastern Europe. The result has been a great opening for religion, including Christian churches. After decades of government-sponsored atheistic propaganda and often severe restriction of religious practice and witness, the thirst of those societies for spiritual meaning and moral security has caused the cup of organized religion to overflow with evangelistic mission and church growth.

NEGATIVE TRENDS

As we approach the year 2000, the negative facts or trends must also be acknowledged. There is strong opposition in most Muslim countries to freedom of religion, religious pluralism, and especially any Christian evangelism. Several of these countries impose, at least in legal theory, the death penalty for "apostasy," which includes Muslim conversion to Christianity. In a country like Saudi Arabia, several hundred thousand Christians lack the right to have a church. Clergy may not even conduct religious services in private homes.

Religious fundamentalism and extremism, with corresponding intolerance, constitutes another negative factor. This mind-set, threatened by modern society and opposed to change and progress, is present in segments of Christianity, Islam, Judaism and Hinduism. It opposes the free exercise of religion, except where the religion happens to be the "true" religion.

The awakening or rebirth of Oriental religions is also problematic. In some countries, Christianity is being pilloried as a hangover of Western imperialism, not as a legitimate religious option.

The growth of nationalism with emphasis on a nation's identification with a majority religion is often inimical to minority religions and religious liberty. Under these circumstances, national sovereignty stands out against universal human rights. This is worrisome.

Another negative factor is the territorial mentality found in Eastern Orthodoxy, which sees with jaundiced religio-political eyes the presence of and evangelism by other churches in what many Orthodox consider their ecclesiastical "hunting preserves."

Opposition to so-called proselytism is growing, especially in the former communist nations of Eastern Europe. Some church leaders feel threatened by Western professional or lay evangelists and oppose winning of adepts from among those who have been baptized as babies, even though they have no living connection with the church and cannot be called believers in any accepted New Testament sense. Other church leaders oppose any evangelism by non-nationals, even when addressed to the totally unchurched. Efforts are currently under way to pass laws and use the police power of the state to restrict proselytism, that is evangelism, especially by relative newcomers on the ecclesiastic scene, including foreigners.

A final negative factor is the "north-south tension" in the field of human rights. Some nations wish to give priority to economic development, even at the price of reducing human rights. Politicians in such third world countries sometimes claim that human rights and religious liberty are a luxury they cannot afford. Crying poverty needs must be given priority, even at the expense of individual freedoms. Some third world leaders now claim that individual human rights, including religious liberty, is a western concept coming from the Enlightenment and promoted by American individualism. They say that in their countries the collective rights of the nation, society, tribe or family are the building-blocks of human rights, not individual rights. This, of course, has ominous implications for religious liberty, inasmuch as individual conscience often finds itself out of step with collective opinion and tradition.

SOME RELIGIOUS LIBERTY VICTORIES

Despite the windows of vulnerability just noted, marvelous religious liberty victories have occurred. The November 16, 1993 Religious Freedom Restoration Act [RFRA] in the United States was such a victory. The Supreme Court, in its cavalier Employment Division v Smith decision (April, 1990), had eliminated the time-honored and demanding "compelling interest" test for determining when government could burden religion the remaining test being simply that the law had to be generally applicable, and not directed at a particular religious group. RFRA restored by Congressional fiat the requirement (often called the Sherbert test) of the harder "compelling interest" standard for government to restrict the exercise of religion.

Another plus for church-state separation in the United States has been several setbacks for legislative efforts to introduce non-public educational vouchers which could be used to pay for education in church schools.

The new and restrictive law on religion in Russia voted in 1993 by the now defunct parliament (specifically an amendment to the 1990 Religious Freedom Act), was not signed into law by President Yeltsin. However, the danger remains. Former Communists, ultra nationalists, some Orthodox and most Muslim leaders in Russia favor a law to restrict the evangelistic activities of foreigners.

In 1993, legal recognition was granted to many Protestant churches in Mexico, which made them eligible to benefit, as does the Catholic Church, from the sweeping religious liberty provisions recently enacted. In order to restrict the influence of the Catholic Church, which had opposed Mexico's independence from Spain and subsequent "revolutionary" developments, the Mexican Constitution for over half a century did not allow churches to operate schools and required all church buildings to belong to the state. But these and other restrictions have now been lifted.

Non-Catholic churches in Spain received legal recognition, for the first time in Spanish history, at the end of 1992. The religious liberty law for Protestants was passed and signed by the king. It guarantees Protestants equal rights, including, in Article 12, the right of Seventh-day Adventists to observe the seventh-day Sabbath.

In Italy, the Roman Catholic Church is no longer the state church, and the SDA Church is listed, like the Catholic Church, on the Italian IRS/Taxation forms as one of four organizations that can receive from the taxpayers, if they so desire, the otto per mille (.8% of taxes) for charitable, welfare, and third world development purposes. Millions of dollars are involved every year! This is remarkable, especially when one remembers that as late as the 1950s there still were discrimination and restrictions at work against Protestant groups and individuals in Italy.

THE SUNDAY LAW PENDULUM

Currently the pendulum seems to be swinging away from Sunday blue laws (work cessation), in both the United States and Canada. Despite the 1961 U.S. Supreme Court decision declaring Sunday laws to be constitutional, if social and not religious as evidenced in both the text and legislative history of the law, a number of states have abolished Sunday laws and others have ignored laws remaining on the books. Only a few states still have effective Sunday closing laws. In Canada, Sunday laws are under attack.

In Britain, also, the trend is away from Sunday laws. On December 8, 1993, the House of Commons, despite strong opposition from the "keep Sunday special" lobby, voted for partial deregulation of the Sunday Trading Act; the bill has been agreed to by the house of Lords. Small shops may now open all day on Sunday, and big stores and supermarkets for up to six hours.

The European Parliament is trying to standardize throughout the European Community the weekly day of rest. It has put into the relevant legislation, however, a statement requiring that in applying the weekly day of rest, "existing religious facts" be taken into account. Among such facts is, of course, the day of rest observed by minorities, such as Adventists and Jews.

Earlier we used the "pendulum" metaphor in referring to Sunday law trends. We need to watch the prophetic clock and be aware of the pendulum swings, without timetabling God and letting our imagination soar into the realm of wishful sensationalism, as some individuals and organizations have been prone to do, at their own peril.

The universe is in the hands of a mighty God, whose purposes know no delay and no defeat. Christians worship a Savior and serve a God of liberty that is what salvation, redemption, and deliverance are all about. Any persecution and suffering are only temporary. When you are on God's side, you are on the winning side and will inevitably bask in "the glorious liberty of the children of God" (Romans 8:21 KJV).

Appendix I

Declaration on Religious Liberty World Council of Churches, Amsterdam, 1948

An essential element in a good international order is freedom of religion. This is an implication of the Christian faith and of the worldwide nature of Christianity. Christians, therefore, view the question of religious freedom as an international problem. They are concerned that religious freedom be everywhere secured. In pleading for this freedom, they do not ask for any privilege to be granted to Christians that is denied to others. While the liberty with which Christ has set men free can neither be given nor destroyed by any Government, Christians, because of that inner freedom, are both jealous of its outward expression and solicitous that all men should have freedom in religious life. The nature and destiny of man by virtue of his creation, redemption and calling, and man's activities in family, state and culture establish limits beyond which the government cannot with impunity go. The rights which Christian discipleship demands are such as are good for all men, and no nation has ever suffered by reason of granting such liberties. Accordingly:

The rights of religious freedom herein declared shall be recognized and observed for all persons without distinction as to race, colour, sex, language, or religion, and without imposition of disabilities by virtue of legal provision of administrative acts.

1. Every person has the right to determine his own faith and creed.

   The right to determine faith and creed involves both the process whereby a person adheres to a belief and the process whereby he changes his belief. It includes the right to receive instruction and education.

   This right becomes meaningful when man has the opportunity of access to information. Religious, social and political institutions have the obligation to permit the mature individual to relate himself to sources of information in such a way as to allow personal religious decision and belief.

   The right to determine one's belief is limited by the right of parents to decide sources of information to which their children shall have access. In the process of reaching decisions, everyone ought to take into account his higher self-interests and the implications of his beliefs for the well-being of his fellowmen.

2. Every person has the right to express his religious beliefs in worship, teaching and practice, and to proclaim the implications of his beliefs for relationships in a social or political community.

   The right of religious expression includes freedom of worship both public and private; freedom to place information at the disposal of others by processes of teaching, preaching and persuasion; and freedom to pursue such activities as are dictated by conscience. It also includes freedom to express implications of belief for society and its government.

This right requires freedom from arbitrary limitation of religious expression in all means of communication, including speech, press, radio, motion pictures and art. Social and political institutions should grant immunity from discrimination and from legal disability on grounds of expressed religious conviction, at least to the point where recognized community interests are adversely affected.

Freedom of religious expressions is limited by the rights of parents to determine the religious point of view to which their children shall be exposed. It is further subject to such limitations, prescribed by law as are necessary to protect order and welfare, morals and the rights and freedoms of others. Each person must recognize the rights of others to express their beliefs and must have respect for authority at all times, even when conscience forces him to take issue with the people who are in authority or with the position they advocate.

3. Every person has the right to associate with others and to organize with them for religious purposes.

    This right includes freedom to form religious organizations, to seek membership in religious organizations, and to sever relationship with religious organizations.

    It requires that the rights of association and organization guaranteed by a community to its members includes the right of forming associations for religious purposes.

    It is subject to the same limits imposed on all associations by non-discriminatory laws.

4. Every religious organization, formed or maintained by action in accordance with the rights of individual persons,

has the right to determine its policies and practices for the accomplishment of its chosen purposes.

The rights which are claimed for the individual in his exercise of religious liberty become the rights of the religious organization, including the right to determine its faith and creed, to engage in religious worship, both public and private, to teach, educate, preach and persuade, to express implications of belief for society and government. To these will be added certain corporate rights which derive from the rights of individual persons, such as the right: to determine the form or organization, its government and conditions of membership; to select and train its own officers, leaders and workers; to publish and circulate religious literature, to carry on service and missionary activities at home and abroad, to hold property and to collect funds; to cooperate and to unite with other religious bodies at home and in other lands, including freedom to invite or to send personnel beyond national frontiers and to give or to receive financial assistance, to use such facilities, open to all citizens or associations, as will make possible the accomplishment of religious ends.

In order that these rights may be realized in social experience, the state must grant to religious organizations and their members the same rights which it grants to other organizations, including the right of self-government, of public meeting, of speech, of press and publications, of holding property, of collecting funds, of travel, of ingress and egress, and generally of administering their own affairs.

The community has the right to require obedience to non-discriminatory laws passed in the interest of public order and well-being. In the exercise of its rights, a religious organization must respect the rights of other religious organizations and must safeguard the corporate and individual rights of the entire community.[1]

Appendix II

Statement on Religious Liberty: World Council of Churches, New Delhi, 1961

Mankind is threatened by many forces which curtail or deny freedom. There is accordingly urgent need to reinvigorate efforts to ensure that every person has opportunity for the responsible exercise of religious freedom.

Christians see religious liberty as a consequence of God's creative work, of his redemption of man in Christ, and his calling of men into his service. God's redemptive dealing with men is not coercive. Accordingly, human attempts by legal enactment or by pressure of social custom to coerce or to eliminate faith are violations of the fundamental ways of God with men. The freedom which God has given in Christ implies a free response to God's love and the responsibility to serve fellow men at the point of deepest need.

Holding a distinctive Christian basis of religious liberty, we regard this right as fundamental for men everywhere.

We affirm the Declaration on Religious Liberty adopted by the World Council of Churches and the International Missionary Council in August-September 1948, and hold to its provisions. We recognize the Universal Declaration of Human Rights, proclaimed by the United Nations in December 1948, as an important instrument in promoting respect for and observance of human rights and fundamental freedoms.

Although freedoms of every kind are interrelated, religious liberty may be considered as a distinctive human right, which all men may exercise no matter what their faith. The article on religious freedom in the Universal Declaration is an acceptable standard, always provided that it be given a comprehensive interpretation.

Everyone has the right to freedom of thought, conscience and religion, this right includes freedom to change his religion or belief, and freedom, either alone or in community with others and in public or private, to manifest his religion or belief in teaching, practice, worship and observance.

The recognition of the inherent dignity and of the equal and inalienable rights of all members of the human family requires that the general standard here declared should be given explicit expression in every aspect of society. Without seeking to be inclusive, we illustrate as follows:

Freedom to manifest one's religion or belief, in public or in private and alone or in community with others, is essential to the expression of inner freedom.

It includes freedom to worship according to one's chosen form, in public or in private.

It includes freedom to teach, whether by formal or informal instruction, as well as preaching with a view to propagating one's faith and persuading others to accept it.

It includes freedom of observance by following religious customs or by participating in religious rites in the family or in public meeting.

Religious liberty includes freedom to change one's religion or belief without consequent social, economic, and political disabilities. Implicit in this right is the right freely to maintain one's belief or disbelief without external coercion or disability.

The exercise of religious liberty involves other human rights. The Universal Declaration proclaims among others, the right to freedom of peaceful assembly and association; the right to freedom of opinion and expression including freedom to seek, receive and impart information and ideas through any media and regardless of frontiers; the prior right of parents to choose the kind of education that shall be given to their children; freedom to participate in choosing the desired form of government and in freely electing officials, freedom from the retroactive application of penal law; and freedom to leave and to return to one's country, and to seek asylum elsewhere.

The freedom with which Christ has set us free calls forth responsibility for the rights of others. The civil freedom which we claim in the name of Christ must be freely available for all men to exercise responsibly. It is the corresponding obligation of government and of society to ensure the exercise of these civil rights without discrimination. It is for the churches in their own life and witness, recognizing their own past failures in this regard, to play their indispensable role in promoting the realization of religious liberty for all men.[2]

Reference Notes

Chapter One

1. Francis Newton Thorpe, The Federal and State Constitutions (Washington: Government Printing Office, 1909), vol. VII, p. 3814.

2. Ibid., vol. V, p. 3082.

3. Thomas Paine, Rights of Man (New York: Willey Book Co., 1942), pp. 33, 34.

4. For a detailed study of this topic see V. Norskov Olsen, Man, the Image of God (Washington, D.C.: Review and Herald Publishing Association, 1988).

5. United Nations Office of Public Information, The International Bill of Human Rights (New York: United Nations, 1978), p. 4.

6. Francis A. Schaeffer, A Christian Manifesto (Westchester, Ill.: Crossway Books, 1981), p. 69.

7. Ellen G. White, Patriarchs and Prophets (Mountain View, California: Pacific Press Publishing Association, 1913), pp. 48 and 331–332.

8. Joseph Baldwin, Psychology Applied to the Art of Teaching (New York: D. Appleton & Co., 1892), pp. 264–266.

9. Arthur Holmes, ed., The Making of a Christian Mind (Downers Grove, Ill.: Inter Varsity Press, 1983), p. 22.

10. Emil Brunner, The Divine Imperative (Philadelphia: Westminster Press, 1957), p. 26.

11. Thomas Merton, No Man is an Island (New York: Harcourt, Brace & World, 1955), p. 27.

12. Emil Brunner, Christianity and Civilization (New York: Charles Scribner's Sons, 1949), Vol. 1, p. 134.

13. Ibid., p. 132.

14. M. Valentine, Natural Theology; or Rational Theism (New York: Silver, Burdett & Co., 1885), p. 26.

15. Arnold Toynbee, An Historian's Approach to Religion (London: Oxford University Press, 1956), p. 205.

16. Eberhard Jüngel, "Toward the Heart of the Matter," in Christian Century, Feb. 27, 1991, p. 233.

Chapter Two

1. See A. F. Carrillo De Albornoz, The Basis of Religious Liberty (London: SCU Press Ltd., 1963), p. 40.

2. Ibid., p. 56.

3. Niels H. Soe, "The Theological Basis of Religious Liberty," in The Ecumenical Review, vol. XI, no. 1 (October 1958), p. 40.

4. Ibid., pp. 41, 42.

5. See A. F. Carrillo De Albornoz, ibid., p. 56.

6. Amos N. Wilder, "Eleutheria for the New Testament and Religious Liberty" in The Ecumenical Review, vol. XIII, No. 4 (July 1961), p. 414.

7. See ibid., pp. 410–411.

8. John R. W. Stott, The Cross of Christ (Downers Grove, Illinois: 1986), pp. 159, 152.

9. G. C. Berkouwer, Sin (Grand Rapids, Michigan: William B. Eerdmans Publishing Company, 1971), p. 199.

10. For a more detailed study see V. Norskov Olsen, ibid., pp. 46–52.

11. See Amos N. Wilder, ibid., p. 411.

12. Ibid., p. 412.

13. See Philip Wogaman, Protestant Faith and Religious Liberty (Nashville: Abingdon Press, 1967), pp. 65–66.

14. Franklin Hamlin Little, The Free Church (Beacon Hill, Boston: Starr King Press, 1957), p. 61.

15. Ellen G. White, The Great Controversy (Mountain View, Ca.: Pacific Press Publishing Association, 1911), p. 493.

16. G. C. Berkouwer, Man: The Image of God (Grand Rapids, Michigan: Wm. B. Eerdmans Publishing Company, 1962), p. 330.

Chapter Three

1. Oscar Cullman, The State In The New Testament (London: SCM Press Ltd, 1963), p. 15.

2. Ibid.

3. Ibid., p. 44.

4. Hans Küng, Freedom Today (New York: Sheed and Ward, 1966), p. 31.

5. Cullmann, ibid., p. 11.

6. Ibid., p. 12.

7. Ibid., p. 46.

8. Ibid.

9. Charles Colson, Kingdoms in Conflict (Zondervan Publishing House, 1987), p. 83.

10. Ibid., pp. 85, 93.

11. Philip Schaff, The Progress of Religious Freedom (New York: Charles Scribner's Sons, 1889), p. 85.

Chapter Four

1. This topic the writer has dealt with at length elsewhere. See V. Norskov Olsen, Papal Supremacy and American Democracy (Loma Linda/Riverside, California: Loma Linda University Press, 1987).

2. Henry Bettenson, ed., Documents of the Christian Church (New York and London: Oxford University Press, 1943), p. 22.

3. Williston Walker, A History of the Christian Church (New York: Charles Scribner's Sons, 1959), p. 105.

4. William A. Dunning, A History of Political Theories, Ancient and Mediaeval (New York: The Macmillan Company, 1913), p. 133.

5. Walker, Ibid., p. 105.

6. Christopher Dawson, The Making of Europe (London: Sheed and Ward, 1953), pp. 27–28.

7. John D. McKnight, The Papacy, A New Appraisal (New York: Rinehart and Co., 1952), p. 181.

8. Alexander C. Flick, The Rise of the Medieval Church (New York: Burt Franklin, 1909), p. 297.

9. Margaret Deanesly, A History of the Medieval Church, 590– 1500, 8th ed. (London: Methuen and Company, Ltd., 1954), p. 9.

10. Thomas Greenwood, Cathedra Petri: A Political History of the Great Latin Patriarchate (London: C. J. Stewart, 1858), book III, chap. IV, p. 135.

11. Ibid., p. 137. See also Flick, ibid., pp. 179– 80.

12. John N. Figgis, Studies of Political Thought from Gerson to Grotius 1414– 1625 (Cambridge: The University Press, 1956), p. 4.

13. Louis Duchesne, trans. A. H. Matthew, The Beginnings of the Temporal Sovereignty of the Popes, A.D. 754– 1073 (London: Kegan Paul, Trench, Trubner and Company, Ltd., 1908), p. 119.

14. James Bryce, The Holy Roman Empire (Boston: Estes and Lauriat, n.d.), p. 175.

15. R. W. Southern, Western Society and the Church in the Middle Ages (Grand Rapids, Michigan: Wm. B. Eerdman Publishing Company, 1970), p. l01. See also Philip Schaff, History of the Christian Church (Grand Rapids, Michigan, 1957), vol. V, pp. 29– 30.

16. Southern, ibid.

17. Schaff, ibid., p. 157. See also Southern, ibid., p. 105.

18. Henry Bettenson, ed., Document of the Christian Church (London: Oxford University Press, 1943), pp. 160, 161.

19. Philip Schaff, History of the Christian Church, vol. V, The Middle Ages, 1049– 1294 (Grand Rapids, Michigan: Wm. B. Eerdmans Publishing Company, 1957), p. 674.

20. Thomas Aquinas, Commentum in IV Libros Sententiarum, in Ewart Lewis, Medieval Political Ideas (London: Routledge and Kegan Paul, 1954), vol. 2, p. 567.

21. Reinhold Seeberg, trans. Charles E. Hay, Textbook of the History of Doctrines (Grand Rapids, Michigan: Baker Book House, 1958), vol. II, p. 146.

22. Marshall W. Baldwin, The Medieval Papacy in Action (New York: The Macmillan Company, 1940), p. 69.

23. T. M. Parker, Christianity and the State in the Light of History (New York: Harper and Brothers, 1955), p. 133.24. A. P. D'Entreves, The Medieval Contribution to Political Thought (Oxford: Oxford University Press, 1939), p. 44.

24. A. P. D'Entreves, The Medieval Contribution to Political Thought (Oxford: Oxford University Press, 1939), p. 44.

25. R. L. Poole, Illustrations of the History of Medieval Thought and Learning (London: Society for Promoting Christian Knowledge, 1920), p. 238.

26. E. Emerton, "The Defensor Pacis of Marsiglio of Padua," in Harvard Theological Studies (Cambridge: Harvard University Press, 1920), vol. VIII, p. 1.

27. Alan Gewirth, Marsilius of Padua (New York: Columbia University Press, 1956), vol. II, p. 431.

28. Ibid., p. 425.

29. Ibid., p. 51.

30. Ibid., p. 103.

31. Gewirth, ibid., vol. I (1951), p. 9.

32. Stephen C. Tornay, Ockham: Studies and Selections (LaSalle, Illinois: The Open Court Publishing Comany, 1938), p. 81.

33 Ewart Lewis, Medieval Political Ideas (London: Routledge and Kegan Paul, 1954), vol. II, p. 607.

34. Ibid., p. 611.

35. Ibid., pp. 606– 607.

36. R. Seeberg, "William of Occam", the New Schaff-Herzog Encyclopedia of Religious Knowledge, vol. VIII, pp. 219–220.

37. William A. Müeller, Church and State in Luther and Calvin (Nashville, Tennessee: Broadman Press, 1954), pp. 37–38.

38. Schaff, ibid., vol. VII, p. 543.

39. Ibid.

40. Karl Holl in Müeller, ibid., p. 34.

41. J. L. Neve, in ibid., p. 166.

42. Martin Luther in M. Searle Bates, Religious Liberty: An Inquiry (New York and London: Harper and Brothers, 1945), p. 155.

43. Philip Melanchthon in J. Warns, Baptism (London: The Paternoster Press, 1957), p. 178.

44. Calvin, Institutes, book IV, chap. 20, par. 4, in Henry Beveridge, trans., Institutes of the Christian Religion by John Calvin (Grand Rapids, Michigan: Wm B. Eerdmans Publishing Company, 1957), vol. 2, pp. 653, 654.

45. Ibid., pp. 673–674.

46. Schaff, ibid., vol. VII, p. 546.

47. Müeller, ibid., pp. 115–116.

48. Philip Schaff, The Progress of Religious Freedom (New York: Charles Scribner's Sons, 1889), pp. 46–47.

49. Frank Maloy Anderson, The Constitutions and Other Selected Documents Illustrative of the History of France 1789–1907 (Minneapolis: The B. W. Wilson Company, 1908), p. 172.

50. Schaff, ibid., p. 63.

51. George Huntston Williams, The Radical Reformation (London: Weidenfeld and Nicolson, 1962), p. 846.

52. A. D. Lindsay, The Modern Democratic State (London: Oxford Universsity Press, 1943), Vol. I, p. 117.

53. Albert Hyma, Christiantiy and Politics (New York: J. B. Lippincott Company, 1938), pp. 239, 241.

Chapter Five

1. Francis Newton Thorpe, ed., The Federal and State Constitutions (Washington: Government Printing Office, 1909), vol. VII, p. 3784.

2. Anson Phelps Stokes, Church and State in the United States (New York: Harper and Brothers, 1950), vol. I, p. 163.

3. Thorpe, Ibid., vol. VII, p. 3802.

4. Sanford H. Cobb, The Rise of Religious Liberty in America (New York: Cooper Square Publishers, 1968), p. 78.

5. William Addison Blakely, American State Papers on Freedom in Religion (Washington, D.C.: The Religious Liberty Association, 1913), pp. 18– 19.

6. Ibid., p. 19.

7. Ibid.

8. Ibid., p. 20.

9. Leo Pfeffer, Church, State and Freedom (Boston: The Beacon Press, 1953), p. 69.

10. Cobb, ibid., pp. 149– 50.

11. Blakely, ibid., pp. 22, 23.

12. Ibid., p. 23.

13. Ibid.

14. Ibid., pp. 23– 24.

15. Ibid., p. 30.

16. Ibid., pp. 51– 52.

17. Ibid., p. 31.

18. Ibid., pp. 17– 21.

19. Cobb, ibid., pp. 70– 71.

20. Stokes, ibid., p. 195

21. Thorpe, ibid., vol. VI, p. 3207.

22. Stokes, ibid., p. 196.

23. Ibid.

24 Ibid., p. 197.

25. Thorpe, ibid., pp. 3212, 3213.

26. Cobb, ibid., p. 436.

27. Thorpe, ibid., vol. VII, pp. 3813, 3814,

28. Ibid., vol. III, p. 1889,

29. Ibid., vol. V, p. 2788.

30. Ibid., p. 3082.

31. Ibid., vol. VI, p. 3222.

32. Ibid., vol. I, p. 537.

33. Cobb, ibid., p. 492.

34. Pfeffer, ibid., p. 98.

35. Blakely, ibid., pp. 83, 84.

36. Ibid., p. 87.

37. Anson Phelps Stokes and Leo Pfeffer, Church and State in the United States (New York: Harper and Row, 1950), p. 55.

38. Pfeffer, ibid., pp. 101– 102.

39. Blakely, ibid., p. 92.

40. Ibid., p. 118.

41. Robert L. Maddox, Separation of Church and State (New Yoark: Crossroad, 1987), pp. 59– 60.

42. Blakely, ibid., p. 119.

43. Stokes, ibid., p. 539.

44. Albert J. Menendez, ed., The First Freedom, (Silver Spring, MD: Americans United for Separation of Church and State, 1985).

45. C. Stanley Lowell and Albert J. Menendez, ed., We Hold These Truths (Silver Spring, MD: Americans United for Separation of Church and State), p. 18.

46. W. E. Gladstone, Gleanings of Past Years (London: John Murray, Albemarle Street, 1879), vol I, p. 218.

47. Lowell and Menandez, ibid., p. 16.

Chapter Six

1. See Main Ecumenical Statements on Principles Concerning Religious Freedom (Geneva: World Council of Churches, 1965), pp. 1–3.

2. Quoted by O. Frederick Nolde, Free and Equal (Geneva: World Council of Churches, 1968), p. 17.

3. See Main Ecumenical Statements, ibid., p. 19.

4. Walter M. Abbott, S.J., General Editor, The Documents of Vatican II (London: Geoffrey Chapman, 1967), p. 675.

5. Ibid., pp. 678–79.

6. Ibid., p. 673.

7. Philip Schaff, The Creeds of Christendom (New York: Harper & Brothers, 1877), vol. II, pp. 217, 219, 227, 232.

8. William J. Wolf, "Religious Liberty" in The Second Vatican Council, ed. Bernard C. Pawley (London: Oxford University Press, 1967), pp. 186, 187.

9. Ibid., pp. 177–78.

10. Ibid., p. 203.

11. Abbot, ibid., p. 677.

12. Wolf, ibid., pp. 192, 193.

13. B. B. Beach, Introduction, "Second World Congress on Religious Liberty Proceedings, September 3– 6, 1984 (Washington, D.C.: International Religious Liberty Association).

14. Main Ecumenical Statements, ibid., p. 37.

15. A. E. Carrillo De Albornoz, "The Ecumenical and World Significance of the Vatican Declaration on Religious Liberty" in "The Ecumenical Review", vol. XVIII, 1966, pp. 61, 63.

16. Abbot, ibid., p. 682.

17. Wolf, ibid., p. 198.

18. Abbot, ibid., p. 685.

19. Ibid.

20. Ibid., p. 683.

21. Quoted by Albert J. Menandez, No Religious Test, (Silver Spring, Maryland: Americans United for Separation of Church and State, 1987), pp. 26– 27.

22. "Universal Declaration of Human Rights" in Human Rights Sourcebook, edited by Albert P. Blaustein, Roger S. Clark, Jay A. Sigler (New York: Paragon House Publishers, 1987), pp. 15– 20.

23. Ibid., pp. 175– 178.

24. Ibid., pp. 163– 165.

25. Ibid., pp. 38– 39.

26. Ibid., pp. 27– 37.

27. Roger S. Clark, "The United Nations and Religious Freedom" in "Journal of International Law and Politics," vol. II, 1978, p. 199.

28. Human Rights Sourcebook, ibid., pp. 63– 66.

29. Philip Schaff, History of the Christian Church (Grand Rapids, Michigan: Wm. B. Eerdmans Publishing Company, (1957), vol. III, p. 380.

30. A. H. Lewis A Critical History of Sunday Legislation (New York: D. Appleton and Company, 1888), p. 36.

31. W. A. Blakely, ed. American State Papers and Related Documents On Freedom and Religion (Washington D.C.: Review and Herald, 1949), p. 379.

32. David N. Laband and Deborah Hendry Heinbucle, Blue Laws: The History, Economics, and Politics of Sunday-Closing Laws (Lexington: D. C. Heath and Comp[any, 1987). pp. 42– 43, 162.

33. Robert Boston, Why The Religious Right is Wrong About Separation of Church and State (Buffalo, New York: Prometheus Books, 1993), p. 167.

34. Pat Robertson, The New World Order (Dallas, London, Vancouver, Melbourn: Word Publishing, 1991), pp. 233– 37.

35. See "Cardinal Law Attacks Sunday-Closing Reform in Massachusetts" in "Church and State", vol. 44, No. 6, 1991, pp. 19– 20.

Appendixes

1. Main Ecumenical Statements On Principles Concerning Religious Freedom (Geneva: World Council of Churches, 1965), pp. 5– 7.

2. Ibid., pp. 35– 37.

About the Author

Born in Denmark, Dr. V. Norskov Olsen later obtained his B.A., M.A., and B.D. from Andrews University, Michigan; a M.Th. from Princeton Theological Seminary; a Ph.D. from the University of London in ecclesiastical history; and a D.Theol. from the University of Basel, Switzerland, in New Testament, Systematic Theology, and Church History.

Dr. Olsen's extensive training and his desire to serve the work of Christ has made him an influential leader on two continents. In Europe, he served as a professor of church history, academic dean, and president at Newbold College, England. In the United States, he served as professor of church history, chair of the Department of Religion, academic dean, provost and from 1974-1984 president of Loma Linda University, California.

At this writing, he was a Scholar in Residence in the Faculty of Religion at Loma Linda University, where he continued his extensive work in research and writing.

We invite you to view the complete
selection of titles we publish at:

www.TEACHServices.com

scan with your mobile
device to go directly
to our website

Please write or email us your praises, reactions, or
thoughts about this or any other book we publish at:

TEACH Services, Inc.
P U B L I S H I N G
www.TEACHServices.com ● (800) 367-1844

Info@TEACHServices.com

TEACH Services, Inc., titles may be purchased in bulk for
educational, business, fund-raising, or sales promotional use.
For information, please e-mail:

BulkSales@TEACHServices.com

Finally if you are interested in seeing
your own book in print, please contact us at

publishing@TEACHServices.com

We would be happy to review your manuscript for free.

www.ingramcontent.com/pod-product-compliance
Lightning Source LLC
Chambersburg PA
CBHW070926270326
41927CB00011B/2746